Practice Tests

Cambridge English
Key *for Schools*

Plus with Key

Rosemary Aravanis

TEACHING NOT JUST TESTING

Pearson Education Limited
Edinburgh Gate
Harlow
Essex CM20 2JE
England
and Associated Companies throughout the world.

http://www.pearsonlongman.com/examsplace

First published 2011
First impression 2016 (without iTest voucher)
Fifth impression 2019
ISBN: 978 1 2921 5956 0

The publisher would like to thank the following for their kind permission to reproduce their photographs:

Alamy Images: Blend Images 118, PhotoAlto 82, Photoshot Holdings Ltd 62; **Fotolia.com:** ArtmannWitte 41, Kadal 59, PETER CLOSE 80, pmphoto 77, redleg 46, Waldo4 113; **Pearson Education Ltd:** Corbis 44, 95, Gareth Boden 98t, Jon Barlow 98b, 116, Sophie Bluy 100, Studio 8 98c, Tudor Photography 10t; **Pearson Education Ltd:** 36; **Rex Features:** Ian Bird 15t, Sipa Press 10; **SuperStock:** Photononstop 64

All other images © Pearson Education

Every effort has been made to trace the copyright holders and we apologise in advance for any unintentional omissions. We would be pleased to insert the appropriate acknowledgement in any subsequent edition of this publication.

Set in Helvetica Neue

Printed in Slovakia by Neografia

Contents

KET for Schools Overview

Paper 1 Reading and Writing (1 hour 10 minutes)	Part 1 – Signs	Questions 1–5 matching task
	Part 2 – Topic vocabulary	Questions 6–10 gapped sentences with three multiple-choice options
	Part 3 – Everyday conversations	Questions 11–15 completing two-line conversations with three multiple-choice options Questions 16–20 completing a longer conversation with a matching task
	Part 4 – Factual text	Questions 21–27 right/wrong/ doesn't say OR three-option multiple choice
	Part 5 – Factual text	Questions 28–35 multiple-choice cloze
	Part 6 – Word completion	Questions 36–40 identifying and writing words
	Part 7 – Notes, short message, letter	Questions 41–50 open cloze
	Part 8 – Information transfer	Questions 51–55 transferring information from input texts to an output text (note, form, etc.)
	Part 9 – Continuous writing	Question 56 guided writing (short message, note or postcard)
Paper 2 Listening (about 30 minutes)	Part 1 – Five short dialogues	Questions 1–5 choosing a picture from three multiple-choice options
	Part 2 – Conversation	Questions 6–10 matching task
	Part 3 – Conversation	Questions 11–15 three-option multiple choice
	Part 4 – Conversation	Questions 16–20 gap fill
	Part 5 – Factual monologue	Questions 21–25 gap fill
Paper 3 Speaking (8–10 minutes)	Part 1 – Personal information	Each candidate interacts with the examiner
	Part 2 – Prompt card activity	The candidates interact with each other

PAPER 1 Reading and Writing Overview

Part 1 – Signs

For **questions 1–5** you read eight short texts (usually signs and notices found in schools, railway stations, airports, shops and on roads, for example) and five sentences that explain the signs and notices. You have to match the five sentences to the eight short texts. Your ability to understand the main message of a sign, notice or other very short text is tested in this part of the paper.

Part 2 – Topic vocabulary

For **questions 6–10** you read five sentences with gaps. The sentences are linked by topic or story line. You have to fill the gap by choosing the best word (A, B or C). These words are verbs, nouns or adjectives. Your ability to read and choose appropriate vocabulary is tested in this part of the paper.

Part 3 – Everyday conversations

For **questions 11–15** you complete five two-line conversations by choosing the best option (A, B or C). For questions 16–20 you complete a longer conversation, by choosing from a list of eight options. There are three extra options that you do not use. The conversations take place in study or social situations. Your ability to understand language used in everyday conversations is tested in this part of the paper.

Part 4 – Factual text

For **questions 21–27** you read one long text or three short texts. The texts are simplified newspaper or magazine articles. You need to answer seven questions. You have to choose between right/wrong/ doesn't say options or choose the right option from A, B or C. Your ability to understand main ideas and some of the details of a longer text are tested in this part of the paper.

Part 5 – Factual text

For **questions 28–35** you read one long text. The text is a simplified newspaper/magazine article or an encyclopaedia entry. The text contains eight gaps and you need to choose the right word from A, B or C to complete the text. Your use of grammar (e.g. verb forms, auxiliary verbs, determiners, pronouns, prepositions and connectives) is tested in this part of the paper.

Part 6 – Word completion

For **questions 36–40** you read five definitions and complete five words, which you have to spell correctly. All the words are related by topic (e.g. food, family and friends, education and free-time activities). They are often nouns but can also be verbs and adjectives. There is one space for each letter of the word. So five spaces means five letters. The first letter of the word is given to you. Your ability to read and identify the right word and your ability to spell that word correctly are tested in this part of the paper.

Part 7 – Notes, short message, letter

For **questions 41–50** you read a short text, usually a note, letter or email, with ten gaps. You have to think of one word to fit each gap. Your use of grammar and vocabulary, as well as your spelling (you must spell the missing word correctly), is tested in this part of the paper.

Part 8 – Information transfer

For **questions 51–55** you read two short texts (e.g. emails, adverts, notes or invitations) and you use the information to complete a short text (e.g. a form, a note or a diary). You have to complete five spaces with one or more words or numbers. Your ability to read and understand short texts and to write down words, phrases or numbers (not sentences) from these texts to complete a different type of text are tested in this part of the paper. Correct spelling is important.

Part 9 – Continuous writing

For **question 56** you write a short message (an email, note or postcard) of 25–35 words. A short text (a note, an email or a postcard) or some instructions will tell you what you need to write. Your ability to communicate a short written message (e.g. a note, email or postcard) to a friend is tested in this part of the paper.

Part 1 – Guidance

Read the instructions and example carefully first.

Read the sentences and short texts carefully. Think about where you might find such signs and notices.

The signs and notices may contain words which you do not know, but this should not stop you from understanding the main message.

You may see the same word appear in a sign/notice and in a sentence. You need to be careful. This does not mean it will be the answer. It is important that you understand the meaning of the sentence in order to be able to match it to a sign/notice.

Part 1 – Practice

1 Read the instructions to the exam task on page 8.

1 How many sentences are there?
2 How many signs and notices are there?
3 Where should you write your answer?

2 Look at the example 0. Why is A the correct answer?

1 Which words in the sign mean *here*?
2 Which words in the sign mean *eat or drink*?

3 Match the three signs with a sentence below. Underline the words that helped you decide.

See this person if you have lost something.
You must be quiet when this is happening.
You should not talk in this place.

No talking during test.	Found – a small black purse – see Ms Smith.	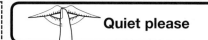 Quiet please

4 Match the modal verbs on the left with their meanings on the right.

can	not able to
cannot	do not
must	need to
must not	it's not a good idea to
should not	it's a good idea to
should	able to

5 Choose the correct modal verb so that the meaning of the sentence is the same as the meaning of the sign.

1	NO EXIT	You cannot/can go out this way.
2	BE ON TIME	You should not/should be late.
3	BE HERE AT 10.00	You must/can be here at this time.
4	VISITING HOURS 4PM – 8PM	You must/must not visit during these times.
5	MOBILE PHONES NOT ALLOWED	You should/should not use your phone here.

Part 1

Which notice (**A–H**) says this (**1–5**)?
For questions **1–5**, mark the correct letter **A–H** on your answer sheet.

Example:

0   You must not eat or drink in here.   *Answer:*

0	A	B	C	D	E	F	G	H
	■	☐	☐	☐	☐	☐	☐	☐

---

1   You should not call out an answer.

A
> NO FOOD OR DRINKS IN THE
> CLASSROOM

2   You must not make any noise.

B
> **Want to say something?**
> **Raise your hand**

3   You must not bring these items of clothing into the classroom.

C
> *Walk don't run*

4   Call this number if you have found something.

D
> **Tennis lessons for kids**
> **Every Saturday morning at 9.00**

5   Be here at this time if you want to learn how to play this sport.

E
> **Hang coats and jackets**
> **in the hall**

F
> **Test in progress**
> **Please be quiet**

G
> *LOST*
> *A black and white pencil case*
> *Call Fiona 0789654334*

H
> **Found something that's not yours?**
> **Tell your teacher.**

Part 2 – Guidance

Read the instructions and the example sentence before you begin. That way you will know the story line or the topic of the sentences.

Read the whole sentence before deciding which word best fits the gap. When you have chosen, read the sentence again to make sure it makes sense.

Part 2 – Practice

1 Verb patterns

Some verbs are followed by *to + infinitive*

want   learn   choose   agree   ask   help   hope   plan   decide

Some verbs are followed by *-ing* or a noun

enjoy   miss   talk about   finish   feel like

Some verbs are followed by both with little difference in meaning.

like   love   prefer   start

Choose the best word. In one sentence both words are possible.

1   I feel like *eating/eat* some chocolate.
2   Joe wants *being/to be* a doctor when he grows up.
3   Have you finished *doing/to do* your homework?
4   I prefer *playing/to play* video games.
5   Jill hopes *doing/to do* well in her exams.

2 Easily confused words

Some words have a similar meaning but they are not used in the same way.

Choose the best word to complete each gap. Put the word in its correct form.

1   come/go/take
    A   'John always .... to school late,' said his teacher.
    B   Penny .... to school by bus.
    C   Louise's mum .... her to school every morning.
2   do/make/play
    A   All she does is .... computer games all day.
    B   Every evening I help to .... the washing-up.
    C   Paul .... his bed every morning before he goes to school.
3   watch/see/look
    A   Did you .... TV last night?
    B   We went to the cinema and .... a very funny film.
    C   Jane has .... everywhere for her keys but she can't find them.
4   already/ever/yet
    A   Have you finished .... ?
    B   She hasn't finished ....
    C   Have you .... seen a baby elephant before?
5   plan/think/decide
    A   This year we .... to visit my cousins in South Africa.
    B   I .... I'll call Rob.
    C   I've .... to write a story about my last holiday.

Part 2

Read the sentences about a boy called Jamie.
Choose the best word (**A**, **B** or **C**) for each space.
For questions **6–10**, mark **A**, **B** or **C** on your answer sheet.

Example:

0   Jamie and his family have just moved to a new ....

     A town   **B** neighbour   **C** countryside   *Answer:*

0	A	B	C
	▬	☐	☐

---

6   Like many kids his age, Jamie enjoys .... video games.

     A doing   **B** making   **C** playing

7   He has made a new .... at school, Paul.

     A boy   **B** student   **C** friend

8   In the morning, Jamie and Paul .... to school on foot.

     A take   **B** come   **C** go

9   They also play football together at the ....

     A weekend   **B** day   **C** afternoon

10   They like spending their .... time together.

     A free   **B** busy   **C** day

Read the instructions and the example before you begin. For questions 16–20, this will help you understand who is talking and where they are.

For questions 11–15 read each question/statement carefully. Think about who might be asking the question or saying the statement and how you might respond to it.

Read each option carefully. When you have decided on an option, read the conversation carefully to make sure it makes sense.

For questions 16–20 read the gapped conversation on the left-hand side first to get an idea of what is said in the conversation.

Read what the first speaker says before and after each gap carefully before deciding on the best response for the gap. When you have completed the dialogue, read it all carefully to make sure it makes sense.

Part 3 – Practice

1 Look at the example on page 12. Why is C the answer?

Is this a yes/no question?

Yes, I am is the short answer for a question beginning with *Are you … ?*

2 Read the questions and statements below and answer these questions.

1 Who do you think is talking? Who are they talking to?
2 What kind of response do you expect for these questions/statements?
3 Can you answer the questions/respond to the statements?
   A Who is Tom talking to?   ....
   B Where do you live?   ....
   C Why are you late?   ....
   D I've got to go now.   ....
   E See you on Thursday.   ....

3 Now, match the responses below to the questions/statements in 2 above.

1 Across the road.
2 But it's early.
3 What time will you be there?
4 Jill's sister, I think.
5 I missed the earlier bus.

4 Read the instructions to the second Part 3 exam task on page 13.

1 Who are the speakers?
2 Where do they have their conversation?

5 Read the gapped conversation without looking at the options.

1 Why is Maria calling?
2 Can Yolanda go out with Maria on Saturday?
3 When will Maria go out with Yolanda?

Part 3

Complete the five conversations.
For questions **11–15**, mark **A**, **B** or **C** on your answer sheet.

Example:

0

---

11 Whose bag is that?

    A Sally's, I think.

    B Yes, it is.

    C It's not me.

12 Let's call Samantha to see what she's doing.

    A Not bad.

    B I hope so.

    C Good idea.

13 How are you feeling?

    A Much better, thank you.

    B I don't think so.

    C I don't feel like it.

14 I have to go and do my homework now.

    A Have you finished?

    B Do you like it?

    C I'll see you later.

15 Why didn't you come to my party?

    A I didn't like it.

    B I wasn't feeling well.

    C I had a great time.

Part 3

Complete the phone conversation between two friends.
What does Yolanda say to Maria?
For questions **16–20**, mark the correct letter **A–H** on your answer sheet.

Example:

| Maria: | Hi, Yolanda. It's Maria. | | |
| Yolanda: | **0** .... D .... | *Answer:* |  |

Maria:	Really? I was calling to see what you were doing on Saturday.	**A**	My mum and I are going shopping. I want to buy some new jeans.
Yolanda:	**16**	**B**	Oh yeah. I forgot about that. Is it this weekend?
Maria:	Oh, I need to get some too. I was thinking about seeing a film.	**C**	I'd love to go. What do you want to see?
Yolanda:	**17**	**D**	I was just going to call you.
Maria:	I can't. I'll be playing in the basketball final.	**E**	Don't worry. I'll be there.
Yolanda:	**18**	**F**	OK. See you then.
Maria:	Yes, and I was hoping you could come.	**G**	I can't come on Sunday.
Yolanda:	**19**	**H**	Maybe we could go on Sunday.
Maria:	Great! I'll see you on Sunday then.		
Yolanda:	**20**		

Part 4 – Guidance

Read the instructions carefully. They tell you what the text is about.
Read the text quickly to get the general meaning. The text will contain words you don't know. Don't worry about these. You can still answer the questions.
Read the example and try to see where the answer is located in the text.
Read the questions carefully and underline the key words. These should help you scan the text to locate the information you need to answer the questions. The questions follow the order of the information in the text, so answer them in order.
Read the text again, more carefully this time, to find answers to the questions.
Answer option 'Wrong' means the information in the text is different from the information in the question. Answer option 'Doesn't say' means that the question asks for information that is not in the text.

Part 4 – Practice

1 Read the instructions and title of the text on page 15.

1 How many questions are there?
2 What do you have to do in this task?
3 What is the text about?
4 Where do you mark your answers?

2 Look at this information. Which do you think will be in the article? Can you guess two more things that might be in the article?

- Jessica's age
- Jessica's hobbies
- Jessica's friends

- a journey
- dates
- places

- ....
- ....

3 Read the text quickly to check your answers to 2 above.

4 Look at the example 0. Why is A the correct answer? Where is the information in the text that supports the statement?

5 Underline the key words in questions 21–27 on page 16.

6 Read the text again and answer questions 21–27. Use these clues to help you.

21 Which city did she leave from? Which city did she return to?
22 What date did she leave on? What date did she return on?
23 Do we know when Jessica's birthday is?
24 How old was Jessica when she sailed around the world? How old was Perham when he did it?
25 How many people were in Sydney the day Jessica returned?
26 What does '2000 nautical miles' refer to in the text?
27 Does Jessica say when she will sail around the world again?

Part 4

Read the article about a young sailor named Jessica Watson.
Are sentences **21–27** 'Right' (**A**) or 'Wrong' (**B**)?
If there is not enough information to answer 'Right' (**A**) or 'Wrong' (**B**), choose 'Doesn't say' (**C**).
For questions **21–27**, mark **A**, **B** or **C** on your answer sheet.

Jessica Watson – a hero

On 18th October 2009, 16-year-old Jessica Watson set out to do
something no one her age had ever done before – to sail around the world
alone without any help. She started her trip in Sydney, Australia, on her
10-metre boat and after 7 long months alone at sea she finally ended up
back in Sydney Harbour on 15th May 2010. As expected, she got a hero's
welcome, with thousands of people there to greet her, including 18-year-
old Mike Perham. Perham had sailed around the world the previous year at the age of 17.

When she was asked why she wanted to make this difficult journey, Jessica simply answered that she
wanted to do something to be proud of. But her trip did not end as well as she had hoped. Instead of
listing her as the youngest person to ever sail around the world alone, the World Speed Sailing Record
Council said she needed to have sailed 2000 nautical miles more than she did to break the world
record. After hearing this, Jessica wrote in her blog, "If I haven't been sailing around the world, then it
beats me what I've been doing out here all this time."

0   Jessica is the youngest person to sail around the world.

A Right   **B** Wrong   **C** Doesn't say   *Answer:*   [0] [A ■] [B □] [C □]

---

21   Jessica started and ended her trip from the same city.

A Right   **B** Wrong   **C** Doesn't say

22   Jessica took a little more than 7 months to complete the journey.

A Right   **B** Wrong   **C** Doesn't say

23   Jessica returned to Sydney on the day of her birthday.

A Right   **B** Wrong   **C** Doesn't say

24   Mike Perham was two years older than Jessica when he sailed around the world.

A Right   **B** Wrong   **C** Doesn't say

25   When Jessica arrived back in Sydney, there were many people there to greet her.

A Right   **B** Wrong   **C** Doesn't say

26   Jessica sailed 2000 nautical miles more than anyone else.

A Right   **B** Wrong   **C** Doesn't say

27   Jessica said she will sail around the world again next year.

A Right   **B** Wrong   **C** Doesn't say

Part 5 – Guidance

Read the instructions carefully. Then read the whole text quickly, to get a general idea of what the text is about.

Read the text again, this time more carefully. Read the whole sentence containing the gap and try to guess what the missing word might be.

Look carefully at the three options and choose the best word.

Read the text a third time, this time with the words in the gaps. Make sure it makes sense.

Part 5 – Practice

1   Read the instructions and title of the text on page 18.

1   What is the text about?
2   How many questions are there?

2   Look at the example 0. Why is A correct?

3   Prepositions
Complete the gaps with a preposition from the box.

in	at	of	by	on	at	on	to	in	to

1   Let's meet .... 6.00 o'clock.
2   I usually go to school .... foot but today I came .... bus.
3   I was born .... the 11th October.
4   Do you go .... primary school?
5   What time do you wake up .... the morning?
6   Can I speak .... you, please?
7   I live .... the house with the red door.
8   At the age .... three, I was able to read and write.
9   Look .... me, I can fly!

4   Pronouns, determiners and quantifiers
Choose the best option.

1   Is that jumper *your/yours*?
2   *Their/There* are many people outside.
3   Is *everyone/someone* all right?
4   I have *many/few* friends – at least 20!
5   *Many/Much* people think maths is hard but I don't.
6   Can I have *a/some* sugar, please?

5   Verb forms
Put the verbs in brackets in the correct form.

1   I have .... (see) that film three times already.
2   We are .... (stay) in a very nice hotel.
3   Yesterday, I .... (go) to the zoo with my class.
4   I really enjoy .... (read) in bed.
5   I .... (go) to judo classes every Monday.

6   Connectives
Choose the best option.

1   I would like to come *and/but* I'm busy on Saturday.
2   I know you like chocolate *so/because* I bought you some.
3   Jane didn't come *and/because* she had already seen the film.
4   Peter washed the car *and/but* did the washing-up too.

Part 5

Read the article about the child actor, Dakota Fanning.
Choose the best word (**A**, **B** or **C**) for each space.
For questions **28–35**, mark **A**, **B** or **C** on your answer sheet.

A child actor

The child actor Dakota Fanning started her acting career at the early age
(0) .... 5. She is different from many young child actors because she
(28) .... continued her success. She has starred in major films
(29) .... *War of the Worlds*, *Charlotte's Web*, *The Cat in the Hat*,
Hound Dog, and more recently in the extremely popular *Twilight* series.
(30) .... people often wonder what life is like for child actors away
from **(31)** .... big screen and the lights. Perhaps it would surprise you
to learn that Dakota is a regular teenager. She is a member of the girl scouts
and is learning **(32)** .... speak French. She loves **(33)** .... films
and even collects dolls. She likes to knit and **(34)** .... also play the violin. And her dream has always
been to be an actor. She doesn't sound much different from most children, does **(35)** .... ?

Example:

0	**A** of	**B** from	**C** at

Answer:

0	**A** ■■■	**B** ☐	**C** ☐

28	**A** is	**B** has	**C** will

29	**A** as	**B** where	**C** like

30	**A** Every	**B** Few	**C** Many

31	**A** a	**B** the	**C** this

32	**A** to	**B** in	**C** from

33	**A** watch	**B** watching	**C** watched

34	**A** must	**B** should	**C** can

35	**A** she	**B** it	**C** they

Part 6 – Guidance

Read the instructions carefully. They give you the topic that the words all relate to. Read each definition carefully. Try to work out if the word is a noun, verb or adjective. Remember, the topic is given to you. It might help you to think of the word in your own language first.

Part 7 – Guidance

Read the whole text first to get the general meaning. Then read the whole sentence containing the gap before deciding on the right word. Think about the type of word it is. When you've finished, read the whole text again to make sure it makes sense. Make sure spell the missing word correctly. Mistakes in spelling are penalised.

Part 6 – Practice

1 **Unscramble these words using the definitions to help you. Then write them in the right place in the table below.**

You can see this in the sky at night.	nomo ....
This is a very high part of the land.	namotinu ....
The day before today.	dytyeraes ....
It is very cold during these months.	riwtne ....
You do this in water when you want to move.	wism ....
You do this with a ball that someone throws to you.	hactc ....
If something does not cost a lot of money it is this.	pahec ....
If a shop is not open it is this.	delosc ....

noun				
verb				
adjective/adverb				

Part 7 – Practice

1 **Vocabulary**
   Read each sentence and decide what kind of word you need in each gap, a noun, a verb or an adjective.

1 Pizza is my .... food – I could eat it every day!
2 The .... time I saw Mina was a month ago.
3 Sharon .... to bed late every Saturday night.
4 I saw an amazing .... at the cinema on Sunday.

2 **Now complete the gaps in 1 with words from the box in their correct form.**

goes	favourite	film	last

3 **Prepositions, pronouns, connectives, articles**

Complete the gaps in these sentences with one word.

1 George lives next .... the school.
2 I watched a football match .... TV last night.
3 Jane told .... to be on time but he didn't listen.
4 Do you know where I put .... ?
5 This is .... you should leave your bag.
6 I might buy this top .... I might buy that one – I can't decide.
7 My house is .... one with the green windows.
8 We made .... delicious cake yesterday.

Part 6

Read the descriptions of some words about family and friends.
What is the word for each one?
The first letter is already there. There is one space for each other letter in the word.
For questions **36–40**, write the words on your answer sheet.

Example:

0   This person is your mum or dad's sister.   a _ _ _

Answer: | 0 | *aunt*

---

36   This is the person who lives next door to you.   n _ _ _ _ _ _ _ _

37   This person is someone you know well and that you like.   f _ _ _ _ _

38   This person is your uncle's child.   c _ _ _ _ _

39   If you have a husband or wife you are this.   m _ _ _ _ _ _

40   This person is invited to visit you in your home.   g _ _ _ _

Part 7

Complete the email message.
Write ONE word for each space.
For questions **41–50**, write the words on your answer sheet.

Example: | 0 | *was* |

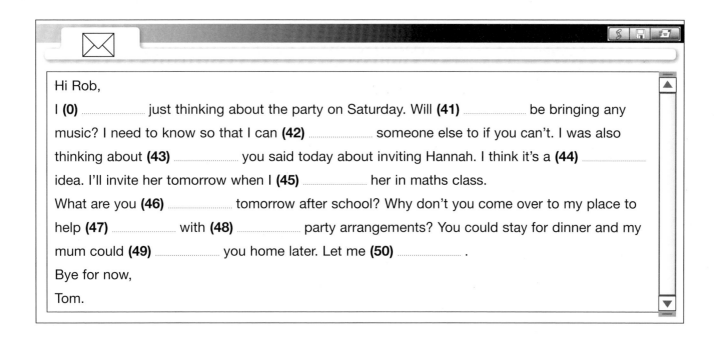

Hi Rob,

I **(0)** .... just thinking about the party on Saturday. Will **(41)** .... be bringing any music? I need to know so that I can **(42)** .... someone else to if you can't. I was also thinking about **(43)** .... you said today about inviting Hannah. I think it's a **(44)** .... idea. I'll invite her tomorrow when I **(45)** .... her in maths class.

What are you **(46)** .... tomorrow after school? Why don't you come over to my place to help **(47)** .... with **(48)** .... party arrangements? You could stay for dinner and my mum could **(49)** .... you home later. Let me **(50)** ....

Bye for now,

Tom.

Part 8 – Guidance

Read the instructions and input texts carefully. Then, look at the example and the writing task carefully.

You need to understand the vocabulary needed to fill in forms or to take notes. For example, name, surname, date of birth, age, address, date, time, cost, etc.

The texts may contain two names, two dates, two prices, etc. Read the texts carefully. You need to make sure you write the correct information in the space.

Correct spelling is important, so make sure you copy the words correctly.

Part 8 – Practice

1 Read the instructions to the task on page 24.

1 What type of texts do you need to read?

2 What type of text do you need to complete?

2 Look at these input texts and completed task. What has the student done wrong? Can you correct his/her work?

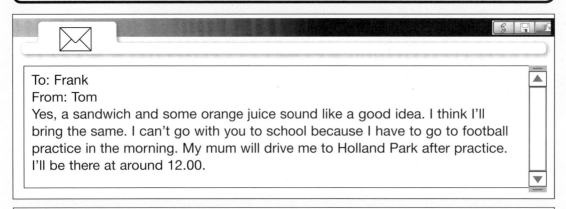

School picnic
Sunday 10th May at Holland Park. Please bring something to eat and comfortable walking shoes. After lunch we will be going on a long walk. Meet outside the school at 11.00 am.

To: Frank
From: Tom
Yes, a sandwich and some orange juice sound like a good idea. I think I'll bring the same. I can't go with you to school because I have to go to football practice in the morning. My mum will drive me to Holland Park after practice. I'll be there at around 12.00.

Frank's notes
Picnic at: *Holland Park*

Day and date:	**51**	10th May
Be at school by:	**52**	12.00
Take to eat and drink:	**53**	sandwich
Remember to wear:	**54**	confotable walking shoes
Activity after lunch:	**55**	football

3 Read the invitation and text on page 24 carefully and answer these questions using words, phrases or numbers. Do not write complete sentences. Underline the parts of the texts that give you the information.

1 Who has written each text? ....

2 Who is having the party? ....

3 When is the party? ....

4 What time is the party? ....

5 Who is Katie going to the party with? ....

6 How will Katie get to the party? ....

7 What time should Katie be at Paul's house? ....

4 Now complete the task on page 24. Remember to use correct spelling.

Part 9 – Guidance

Read the instructions and/or input text carefully. They tell you what type of message you need to write, who it is for and what kind of information you should include. There will always be three things that you will need to communicate in your answer.

If there are only instructions, you must address the prompts in order.

If there is a short input text, you must respond appropriately to all three elements it contains.

You need to write between 25 and 35 words, so count them carefully.

Part 9 – Practice

1 Read the instructions and email on page 24 and answer the questions.

1 Who are you writing to?
2 What type of text do you need to write?
3 What three questions should you answer?

2 Read Michael's email below and the two answers from Ruth and Monica, then answer the questions.

1 Have the students answered all three questions correctly?
2 Have the students written 25–35 words?
3 Which one is better? Why?

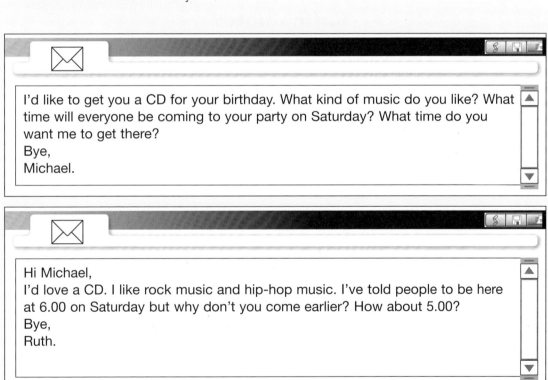

I'd like to get you a CD for your birthday. What kind of music do you like? What time will everyone be coming to your party on Saturday? What time do you want me to get there?
Bye,
Michael.

Hi Michael,
I'd love a CD. I like rock music and hip-hop music. I've told people to be here at 6.00 on Saturday but why don't you come earlier? How about 5.00?
Bye,
Ruth.

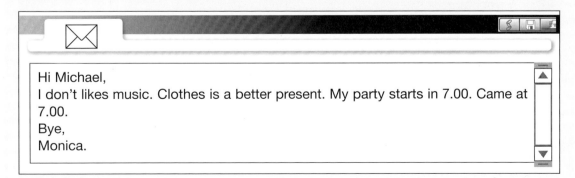

Hi Michael,
I don't likes music. Clothes is a better present. My party starts in 7.00. Came at 7.00.
Bye,
Monica.

Part 8

Read the invitation and the text message.
Fill in the information in Katie's notes.
For questions **51–55**, write the information on your answer sheet.

> *You are invited to my 12th birthday party*
> *on Sunday 14th May.*
> *The party starts at 1 p.m.*
> *My address is:*
> *63 Porter Street*
> *Let me know if you can come by Friday.*
> *Hope to see you there.*
> *Gina.*

Katie, are you going to Gina's party on Sunday? Can we go together? Come to my house at 12.30 and my mum can drive us there. She can also pick us up afterwards. Let me know.
Paul.

Katie's notes

Person having party: Gina

Day and date:	**51**
Time:	**52**
Going with:	**53**
Travel there by:	**54**
Be at Paul's at:	**55**

Part 9

Read this email message from your friend Matt.

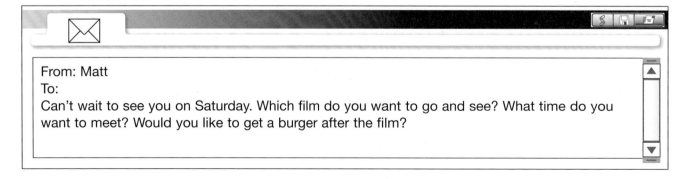

From: Matt
To:
Can't wait to see you on Saturday. Which film do you want to go and see? What time do you want to meet? Would you like to get a burger after the film?

Write an email to Matt and answer the questions.
Write **25–35** words.
Write the email on your answer sheet.

PAPER 2 Listening Overview

Part 1 – Five short dialogues

For **questions 1–5** you listen to five short informal conversations. They are between friends or relatives, or they might take place in a shop, etc. You have to answer five questions by choosing the correct picture (A, B or C). You will hear each conversation twice. Your ability to understand simple facts and important information in a conversation (e.g. prices, numbers, times, dates, locations, directions, shapes, sizes, weather, descriptions of people and actions) is tested in this part of the paper.

Part 2 – Conversation

For **questions 6–10** you listen to a longer conversation. The conversation is an informal one between people who know each other well. The speakers will talk about things that interest them personally (e.g. daily life, travel, free-time activities, etc.). You have to match two lists of items, for example, people with food they like to eat, or days of the week with activities, etc. You will hear the conversation twice. Your ability to understand key information in the conversation is tested in this part of the paper.

Part 3 – Conversation

For **questions 11–15** you listen to a longer conversation. The conversation may be an informal one (e.g. between people who know each other well) or a neutral one (e.g. like those that take place in a shop). You have to answer five questions by choosing A, B or C. You will hear the conversation twice. Your ability to understand key information in the conversation (e.g. numbers, addresses, places, times, dates, names, prices, etc.) is tested in this part of the paper.

Part 4 – Conversation

For **questions 16–20** you listen to a longer neutral or informal dialogue (e.g. in shops, schools, etc.). There are five gaps that you have to fill in with one or two words or numbers. If you misspell a word, your answer will still be accepted, as long as the word is recognisable. However, for common words (e.g. bus, red, etc.) the spelling must be correct. This is also true of words such as names that are spelled out on the recording by the speaker. Your ability to listen and write down specific information (e.g. numbers, times, dates, prices, spellings and words) is tested in this part of the paper.

Part 5 – Factual monologue

For **questions 21–25** you listen to a longer neutral or informal monologue (e.g. in shops, schools, etc.). There are five gaps that you have to fill in with one or two words or numbers. If you misspell a word, your answer will still be accepted as long as the word is recognisable. However, for common words (e.g. bus, red, etc.) the spelling must be correct. This is also true of words, e.g. names, that are spelled out on the recording by the speaker. Your ability to listen and write down specific information (e.g. numbers, times, dates, prices, spellings and words) is tested in this part of the paper.

Part 1 – Guidance

Read the instructions, example and questions carefully.
Look at the pictures carefully and try to guess what information you will hear.
When you listen to the conversation, you may hear the speakers mention all three answers, but only one correctly answers the question.
The second time you listen, check that the answers you chose during the first listening are correct.

Part 1 – Practice

1 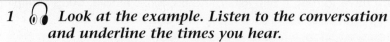 *Look at the example. Listen to the conversation and underline the times you hear.*

John: Hi Jane. It's John here. Just ringing to find out what time we're meeting tonight.

Jane: Hi John. I thought we said at six.

John: No, I can't then. I won't be home till quarter past six. The earliest I can meet is around half past six.

Jane: The film doesn't start till seven. How about we meet at quarter to seven?

John: OK. See you then.

2 *Why is answer C correct? Why are answers A and B wrong?*

3 *Read these questions and underline the important words. Can you think of three possible answers for each question?*

1 How much did the girl pay for her shoes?
2 Which notebook is Jo's?
3 How many children are in Pam's class?
4 Which sport will the boy play on Saturday mornings?
5 What will the girl eat for dinner tonight?

4 *Now check your guesses on pages 27–28. Did you get any of them right?*

5 *Listen and tick the numbers, prices and times you hear.*

1 a 5   b 25
2 a 330   b 303
3 a £14   b £40
4 a £5.99   b £599
5 a 6.45   b 7.15
6 a 7.20 am   b 7.20 pm

6 *In pairs, practise saying the numbers, prices and times in Exercise 5 above.*

7 *Do you know the names of these shapes? Label the pictures.*

1 ☆   2 △   3 ▢   4 ▭   5 ○

8 *In pairs, describe the pictures in Question 2 on page 27.*

9 *Do you know the names of the sports and foods in Questions 4 and 5?*

Part 1

You will hear five short conversations.
You will hear each conversation twice.
There is one question for each conversation.
For each question, choose the right answer (**A**, **B** or **C**).

Example: What time will the boy and girl meet?

A

B

Ⓒ

---

1   How much did the girl pay for her shoes?

A

B

C

2   Which notebook is Jo's?

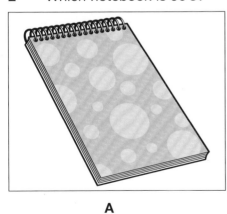
A

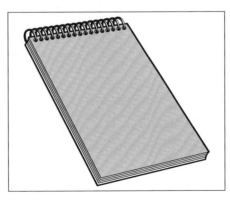
B

C

3   How many children are in Pam's class?

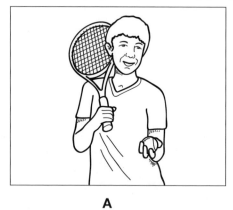

A

B

C

4   Which sport will the boy play on Saturday mornings?

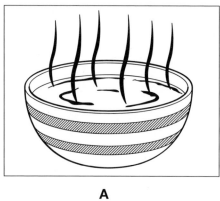

A

B

C

5   What will the girl eat for dinner tonight?

A

B

C

Part 2 – Guidance

Read the instructions, example and lists of items carefully. This way you will know what the speakers will talk about.

You may hear the speakers mention all eight items in the second list but only five match the items in the first list. Three items in the second list do not match the items in the first list. They are distracters. Make sure you listen carefully to what the speakers say. When you listen to the conversation, you should listen out for the items in the first list (e.g. the days of the week, the people's names, etc.) When you hear them, it is a signal that the answer to the question comes next.

The items in the second list appear in alphabetical order. This makes it easier for you to find them when you hear them.

The second time you listen, check that the answers you chose during the first listening are correct.

Part 2 – Practice

1 *Make a list of activities you do when you are on school holidays.*

2 *Look at the task on page 30. Do you see any of your activities in the second list?*

3 *Read the instructions and look again at the task on page 30. Answer these questions.*

1 How many people will be talking?
2 What are the names of the speakers?
3 How do the speakers know each other?
4 What will the speakers talk about?
5 Which of the two speakers will do these activities on the holidays?

4 *Read the Part 2 extract below and underline the people that the speakers mention.*

Kate: I'm going to buy my brother a T-shirt. I was going to buy my sister a book but she said she didn't want one this year, so I think I'll get her a CD.

Paul: What are you going to get your mum?

Kate: I'm not sure. I bought her a purse last year. This year I think I'll get her some flowers.

Brother	book
Sister	CD
Mum	flowers
	purse
	T-shirt

5 *Now match the people on the left in the table in Exercise 4 with a present on the right. Highlight the answers in the extract.*

6 *Which two presents are the distracters?*

Part 2

Listen to Pete talking to a friend about his school holiday plans.
What is he doing each day in the second week of his holidays?
For questions **6–10** write a letter **A–H** next to each day.
You will hear the conversation twice.

Example:

0   Monday   **B**

	DAYS			**PLANNED ACTIVITIES**
6	Tuesday	☐	**A**	cinema
7	Wednesday	☐	**B**	day trip
8	Thursday	☐	**C**	football
9	Friday	☐	**D**	homework
10	Saturday	☐	**E**	no plans
			F	shopping
			G	swimming
			H	theatre

Part 3 – Guidance

Read the instructions, example and questions carefully. This way you will know what the speakers will talk about.

Try to guess the information you will hear.

You may hear the speakers mention all three answer options, but only one will be correct.

The second time you listen, check that the answers you chose during the first listening are correct.

Part 3 – Practice

1 *Read the instructions, example, questions and answer options on page 32. Then answer these questions.*

1 Who are the speakers?
2 What will they be talking about?
3 What information will they mention during their conversation?

2 *Read the questions on page 32 more carefully and underline the key information you have to listen out for.*

3 *Which of the following extracts contains the information needed to complete this sentence?*

Darren and Maria have to write a ... ?

1 Have you started your book report yet?
2 Include a short summary of the story.
3 I haven't actually read the book yet.

4 *Which of these answers is the correct way to complete the sentence in Exercise 3?*

A book report.
B book.
C story.

5 🎧 *Listen to the following dates? Then listen again and repeat.*

20th November
2nd November
12th November
1st December
25th March
31st May

Part 3

Listen to Darren talking to a friend about a book report he has to write for school.
For each question, choose the right answer (**A**, **B** or **C**).
You will hear the conversation twice.

Example:

0   Darren and Maria have to write a

    (**A**) book report.

    B book.

    C story.

---

11   How much of the book has Darren read?

    A all of it

    B none of it

    C half of it

12   The name of the book is

    A *Flight 221.*

    B *Flight 211.*

    C *Flight 212.*

13   Darren returned to school on

    A 20th November.

    B 2nd November.

    C 12th November.

14   When will Darren read the book?

    A tonight.

    B at the weekend

    C next week

15   On Sunday, Darren will call Maria at

    A 6.00.

    B 7.15.

    C 7.00.

Part 4 & 5 – Guidance

Read the instructions, example and notes carefully. This way you will know what the speakers will talk about.

Try to guess the type of information that is missing from the gaps.

The second time you listen, check that the answers you wrote during the first listening are correct. Check also that you have written the name that is spelled out by the speaker correctly.

Check that your spelling of common words are correct.

Parts 4 & 5 – Practice

1 Read the notes for Part 4. What kind of information is missing? Match the questions with A–E below.

Question 16	A a price
Question 17	B a time
Question 18	C a name
Question 19	D a day of the week
Question 20	E a phone number

2 In pairs, try to guess what kind of information is missing for questions 21–25 in Part 5.

3 🎧 Write down the phone numbers you hear.

1 ....
2 ....
3 ....
4 ....

4 In pairs, practise reading out the phone numbers.

5 🎧 Write down the prices you hear.

1 £ ....
2 ....p.
3 £ ....
4 £ ....

6 In pairs, practise reading out the prices.

7 🎧 Listen to some people spelling their names. Write down what you hear.

1 ....
2 ....
3 ....
4 ....
5 ....

8 Work in pairs. Ask your partner to spell the following names:

e.g.   What's your name? – It's Peter.
        How do you spell it? – P.E.T.E.R

Your name: ....
Your dad's/mum's name: ....
Your best friend's name: ....
Your grandmother's name: ....
The name of your town/village ....

Part 4

You will hear a boy asking about an electronic device.
Listen and complete each question.
You will hear the conversation twice.

MP3 Player

The discount is:	20%
Price with discount:	(16) £ ....
Pay for it on:	(17) ....
Come in before:	(18) .... o'clock
Customer's name:	(19) Jack ....
Address:	16 Bond Street
Phone number:	(20) ....

Part 5

You will hear a teacher talking about a school concert.
Listen and complete each question.
You will hear the information twice.

School Concert

Name of school band:	As You Like It
Day of concert:	(21) ....
Be there by:	(22) .... pm
Band practice:	(23) .... and Thursday at 4.00 pm
Room:	(24) ....
If you can't come, call:	(25) ....

PAPER 3 Speaking Overview

You will take the speaking test with another candidate (i.e. in pairs). On rare occasions, three candidates may be tested together. There will always be two examiners in the room with you. One will speak to you and assess you (the interlocutor) and the other will only assess you (the examiner).

In the speaking test, you are not expected to produce completely accurate or fluent language, but you are expected to be able to interact appropriately and intelligibly.

Part 1 – Personal information

You will talk to the examiner by answering his/her questions. The examiner asks you questions about your life. Your ability to answer questions about your life (to give information of a factual personal kind) is tested in this part of the paper. You will need to show you have the language needed to talk to people when you meet them for the first time.

Part 2 – Prompt card activity

You will talk to your partner (i.e. the other candidate). The examiner will set up the activity. You and your partner will ask and answer questions using information given in the prompt material that the examiner will give you. Your ability to give factual information of a non-personal kind related to daily life is tested in this part of the paper.

 Watch the full test on your DVD.

Part 1 – Guidance

Listen to the examiner's questions carefully.

If you don't understand a question, ask the examiner to repeat it. Say *Can you repeat the question, please?* or *Please repeat the question.*

Try to answer questions about yourself using more than one word.

If a question begins with 'Tell us about …' extend your answer even more. Say as many things as you can about the topic.

When you are preparing, it will help you to record yourself, so that you can hear what you have done well and what you need to do better.

Part 1 – Practice

1   *Spelling*
   Practise saying the names of the letters of the alphabet.

A B C D E F G H I J K L M N O P Q R S T U V W X Y Z

2   🎧 *Listen and choose the correct spelling for each name you hear.*

1   Sweny/Sweeney
2   Armstrong/Irnstrong
3   Charlene/Charleen
4   Moneypenny/Moneypeny

3   *In pairs, practise spelling out the names. Then practise spelling your surname.*

4   *Giving personal information. Match the answers to the questions.*

1	What's your name?	a	Chemistry because I don't understand it.
2	What's your surname?		
3	How do you spell that?	b	G.O.L.G.A.N.O.
4	Sorry, can you please repeat that?	c	It's Golgano.
5	What do you do in your free time?	d	Maths, because it's easier than the other subjects.
6	How often do you play football?		
7	What subject do you like best? Why?	e	Every Sunday.
8	What subject is the most difficult?	f	I play football and I watch TV.
		g	G.O.L.G.A.N.O.
		h	My name's Fabio.

5   *Now, in pairs, ask and answer the questions about yourselves.*

6   *School subjects*
   How do you pronounce these school subjects?

Chemistry   Physics   English   History   Maths
French   Geography   Biology   Science

7   🎧 *Listen and check the school subjects and then listen and repeat.*

8   *Which of the school subjects do you do at school? Which do you like best/ least? Why?*

If you are answering questions, listen to your partner's questions carefully. If you don't understand any questions, it is important that you ask your partner to repeat it or say 'I'm sorry I don't understand' (see other things you can say below).

Make sure you look at all the information on the card. The questions your partner asks you will not be in the same order as the information that appears on your card.

If you are asking questions, try to form clear questions that your partner will understand. Use question words like *When? What? Where? How?* etc. to form your questions based on the task card (see example below).

When you are preparing, it will help you to record yourself, so that you can hear what you have done well and what you need to do better.

Singing lessons

- where/lessons?

- what/time?

- cost?

- address?

- telephone number?

1   Can you correct the mistakes in this student's questions?

1   Where the lessons? ....
2   What time the lessons are? ....
3   How much cost the lessons? ....
4   What address? ....
5   Can you tell the telephone number? ....

2   Which of the following can you say if you haven't understood a question? Which two should you not say? Why not?

1   Sorry, I don't understand?
2   What?
3   I don't understand you!
4   Can you please repeat your question?
5   I'm sorry. Please repeat.
6   What do you mean?

Part 1

In class

Work in pairs. Take turns to ask and answer these questions.

1   What's your name?

2   Can you spell your surname for me, please?

3   What school do you go to?

4   Which subjects do you like best?

5   What do you do at the weekends.

At home

Answer the questions on your own. You might want to record yourself so that you can play it back and hear yourself speak. What did you do well? What do you need to work on?

Part 2

Candidate A

A,   here is some information about **an athletics club**. (Turn to page 140)

B,   you don't know anything about **the athletics club**, so ask **A** some questions about it.

Athletics club

- name/club?

- for children?

- website?

- when/training?

- address?

Candidate B

B,   here is some information about **a music school**. (Turn to page 142)

A,   you don't know anything about **the music school**, so ask **B** some questions about it.

Alan's music school

- where/school?

- what/learn?

- cost?

- when/classes?

- phone number?

Part 1

Questions 1–5

Which notice (**A–H**) says this (**1–5**)?
For questions **1–5**, mark the correct letter **A–H** on your answer sheet.

Example:

0   You may be late.

Answer:

0	A	B	C	D	E	F	G	H
	▬	☐	☐	☐	☐	☐	☐	☐

1   You must not come in here.

A   DELAYS POSSIBLE

2   You must not walk on here.

B   **Talk to people the way you would like people to talk to you**

3   You can use these if you pay.

C   *Keep out*

4   You can do this after a certain time.

D   *Keep off the grass*

5   You should be nice.

E   **Chinese lessons every Monday 3.30–5.30**

F   **Boats for hire £10 for 30 minutes**

G   **School library** Use your student card to borrow books

H   *No skateboarding during school times*

> **Exam tip**   *Read all the signs and notices carefully. Try to imagine where you might find them. Then read each sentence carefully. The one you choose should have exactly the same message as the sign or notice.*

Part 2

Read the sentences about a sports club.
Choose the best word (**A**, **B** or **C**) for each space.
For questions **6–10**, mark **A**, **B** or **C** on your answer sheet.

Example:

0   A new sports club has just opened .... Harold's school.

    A near   **B** next   **C** close

Answer:

0	A	B	C
	■	☐	☐

---

6   At the club, you can play your .... sports, like basketball and table tennis.

    A good   **B** favourite   **C** popular

7   There is a café where you can .... something to eat or drink.

    A take   **B** buy   **C** do

8   Harold has already become a .... of the club.

    A member   **B** person   **C** athlete

9   He has tried all .... of sports and activities.

    A forms   **B** kinds   **C** things

10   He .... that the sport he likes the most is table tennis.

    A tells   **B** thinks   **C** says

Exam tip	*When you have chosen an answer, read the whole sentence again with the answer. Does it make sense?*

Part 3

Complete the five conversations.
For questions **11–15**, mark **A**, **B** or **C** on your answer sheet.

Example:

0

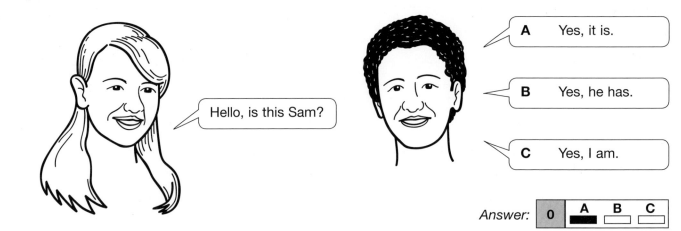

A   Yes, it is.

B   Yes, he has.

C   Yes, I am.

Hello, is this Sam?

Answer:

0	A	B	C
	■	☐	☐

---

11   Where is the nearest newsagent?

    A   I don't think so.

    B   It's over there.

    C   I didn't see it.

12   I really love the summer.

    A   I know you have.

    B   I can't.

    C   So do I.

13   Do you want to go and see a film?

    A   That's a good idea.

    B   I don't know it.

    C   I saw it yesterday.

14   What did you say?

    A   Nothing.

    B   Sometimes.

    C   Anything.

15   Can you hear that noise?

    A   I wonder what it is?

    B   Are you listening?

    C   I haven't heard anything.

Exam tip	*Read the first half of the conversation carefully. Try to imagine how someone might respond. Then read each answer option carefully before choosing an answer.*

Part 3

Complete the conversation between a teacher and a student.
What does the teacher say to Wendy?
For questions **16–20**, mark the correct letter **A–H** on your answer sheet.

Example:

Teacher: Wendy, have you finished your project?

Wendy: **0** .... *A* ....

Answer:

Teacher:	Does that mean you don't have it for me?	**A**	Actually, I need to speak to you about that.
		B	That's just it. I haven't finished it yet.
Wendy:	**16**		
		C	Thanks, Miss. Don't worry I'll have it for you by then.
Teacher:	Can I ask why?		
Wendy:	**17**	**D**	I don't have a computer.
Teacher:	Don't tell me you lost the project.	**E**	Don't worry. I can be there on Monday.
		F	That shouldn't be a problem.
Wendy:	**18**		
		G	I did! I started it again but I haven't finished it yet.
Teacher:	OK. Don't worry. Can you have it for me on Monday?		
Wendy:	**19**	**H**	I would have finished it yesterday but my computer crashed.
Teacher:	Good. I'll expect it bright and early Monday morning.		
Wendy:	**20**		
Teacher:	I hope so!		

> **Exam tip** *Read all the gapped conversation on the left-hand side first. Try to guess what the other person may have said. Then read the line before and after the gap carefully before you choose your answer.*

Questions 21–27

Read the article about three television shows and then answer the questions.
For questions **21–27**, mark **A**, **B** or **C** on your answer sheet.

The Artist in You

The Artist in You is a new show for kids and teenagers. Each week, Tony Moldino, an artist himself, shows you how to make an amazing work of art. Last week, it was painting a portrait. This week it's drawing with pencil on paper, and next week it's how to use your digital camera to take great pictures. It's on every Tuesday at 5.00 pm.

Dance School

Dance School is a new teen drama about a group of students who all want to become dancers. It follows their lives in a school for dancers in New York. The story is told through the eyes of Tina Giles, a farm girl who dreams of becoming a ballerina. On her first day at the school she meets Joe, Heather and John. Together they try hard to achieve their dream. *Dance School* is on every Monday night at 7.00.

Bert

Bert is a new comedy cartoon series for older kids. It follows the funny times of Bert and his family in a small town in America. Each episode is a new story. In this week's episode, Bert's younger sister gets a part in the school play. Bert isn't happy because he too wants to be in the play. He does everything he can think of to get his wish! *Bert* is on every Wednesday at 6.00.

Example:

0   *The Artist in You*

A began this year.   **B** is an old show.   **C** is a show for artists.

Answer:

---

21   Every week on the show *The Artist in You*, you can

A learn to draw.   **B** learn to paint.   **C** learn something new.

22   Tony Moldino is on the show

A this week only.   **B** every week.   **C** next week only.

23   *Dance School* is a show about

A a girl called Tina Giles.   **B** a new school.   **C** a group of young dancers.

24   Tina Giles grew up

A in a city.   **B** in a village.   **C** on a farm.

25   Tina met her school friends for the first time

A on a farm.   **B** at her new school.   **C** years ago.

26   *Bert* is a show about

A students.   **B** a family.   **C** an American town.

27   Bert is unhappy because

A his sister is in the school play.   **B** he isn't in the school play.   **C** he doesn't like school.

> **Exam tip**
> *To answer multiple-choice questions, read the question carefully, but not the options. Find the information in the text. Then look at the answer options and choose the best one. The question and answer option together should say the same thing as the information in the text.*

Part 5

Read the article about the Tasmanian devil.
Choose the best word (**A**, **B** or **C**) for each space.
For questions **28–35**, mark **A**, **B** or **C** on your answer sheet.

The Tasmanian devil

The Tasmanian devil is an unusual animal found only **(0)** .... the island of
Tasmania in the southeast of Australia. **(28)**............... people know the devil from
the popular cartoon character, Taz, but this little animal is in fact a real animal.
What does a real devil look **(29)**............... ? It is the size of a small black dog
and just as cute. **(30)** .... don't let its size fool you. The devil can bite!

In the wild, it is a carnivore, which means it **(31)**............... eat other animals. It **(32)**............... not often
kill the animals it eats though. Rather, it eats animals that have **(33)**............... died from some other cause.

Like many other Australian animals, these little black animals are marsupials. This means **(34)** ....
like kangaroos, for example, they carry their babies in a pouch. Surprisingly, the mother devil
(35)............... look after four little babies at a time!

Example:

0	**A** on	**B** in	**C** at	*Answer:*	0	A ■ B □ C □

28	**A** Every	**B** Each	**C** Most
29	**A** as	**B** like	**C** of
30	**A** But	**B** And	**C** So
31	**A** has	**B** must	**C** will
32	**A** does	**B** do	**C** doing
33	**A** since	**B** yet	**C** already
34	**A** which	**B** that	**C** when
35	**A** does	**B** has	**C** can

> **Exam tip**
> *Read the whole text first to understand the general meaning. Then read the whole sentence containing the gap BEFORE choosing an answer. Finally, read the whole sentence with the answer. Does it make sense?*

Part 6

Read the descriptions of some things that you can find at school and at home.
What is the word for each one?
The first letter is already there. There is one space for each other letter in the word.
For questions **36–40**, write the words on your answer sheet.

Example:

0   This is the place where you have your lessons.   c _ _ _ _ _ _ _ _

<table>
<tr><td>Answer:</td><td>0</td><td>classroom</td></tr>
</table>

---

36   This is what you study at school.   s _ _ _ _ _ _

37   In some schools, students have to wear this.   u _ _ _ _ _ _

38   This person helps you learn things.   t _ _ _ _ _ _

39   You do this study away from school.   h _ _ _ _ _ _ _

40   If you don't know a word, you can look it up in this.   d _ _ _ _ _ _ _ _ _

Exam tip	*Remember to think about the part of speech the word is – the words are usually nouns but they can also be verbs and adjectives. The word should fit the spaces and you need to make sure you spell it correctly.*

Part 7

Complete these emails.
Write ONE word for each space.
For questions **41–50**, write the words on your answer sheet.

Example: | **0** | *where* |

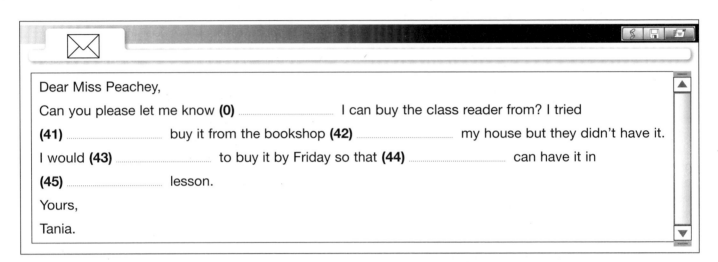

Dear Miss Peachey,

Can you please let me know **(0)** .... I can buy the class reader from? I tried

(41) .... buy it from the bookshop **(42)** .... my house but they didn't have it.

I would **(43)** .... to buy it by Friday so that **(44)** .... can have it in

(45) .... lesson.

Yours,

Tania.

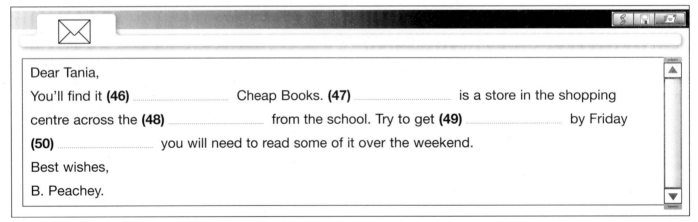

Dear Tania,

You'll find it **(46)** .... Cheap Books. **(47)** .... is a store in the shopping

centre across the **(48)** .... from the school. Try to get **(49)** .... by Friday

(50) .... you will need to read some of it over the weekend.

Best wishes,

B. Peachey.

| Exam tip | *Remember to write only one word in each gap. When you've finished, read the text(s) again together with the answers. Does it make sense? Make sure you write your answers on the answer sheet clearly.* |

Questions 51–55

Read the school notice and the email.

Fill in the information in the application form.

For questions **51–55**, write the information on your answer sheet.

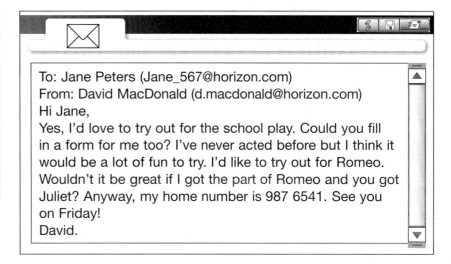

School play Romeo and Juliet
Are you interested in trying out for the school play? Come to room 24B on Friday at 3.30 pm. Complete the form below and bring it with you on Friday.

To: Jane Peters (Jane_567@horizon.com)
From: David MacDonald (d.macdonald@horizon.com)
Hi Jane,
Yes, I'd love to try out for the school play. Could you fill in a form for me too? I've never acted before but I think it would be a lot of fun to try. I'd like to try out for Romeo. Wouldn't it be great if I got the part of Romeo and you got Juliet? Anyway, my home number is 987 6541. See you on Friday!
David.

School play application form

Name of play:	Romeo and Juliet
Full name:	**51**
Acting experience:	**52**
Part trying out for:	**53**
Phone number:	**54**
Email address:	**55**

> **Exam tip** *When you've finished, make sure you check your answers carefully. Look back at the input texts to check you have copied the answers correctly.*

Part 9

Question 56

You are going out. Leave a note for your parents. Tell them:

- **where** you are going.
- **who** you are going with.
- **what time** you will be home.

Write **25–35** words.

Write the note on your answer sheet.

> **Exam tip** Write your notes or answers next to the bullet points or questions before you write your reply. That way you will not forget to mention something and you will remember to mention everything in the correct order. Don't forget to check your writing carefully (and count your words). If you make any changes, you may need to rewrite your reply so that it's clear.

Part 1

Questions 1–5

You will hear five short conversations.
You will hear each conversation twice.
There is one question for each conversation.
For each question, choose the right answer (**A**, **B**, or **C**).

Example: Where did the boy go on holiday?

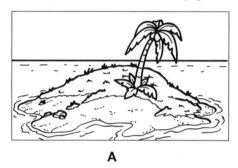

A

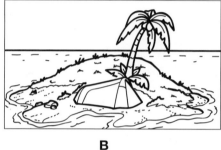

B

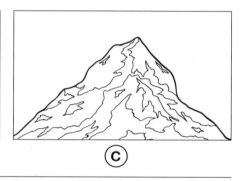

C

1 What's the weather going to be like tomorrow?

A

B

C

2 Where are the boys going to meet their friend?

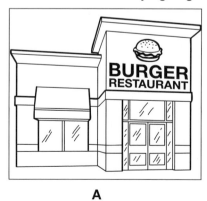

A

B

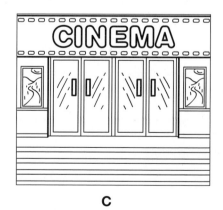

C

3 Which card does Nicole buy?

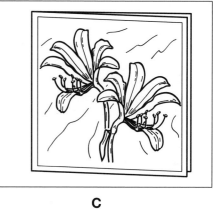

A   B   C

4 How many chocolate ice creams does the boy want?

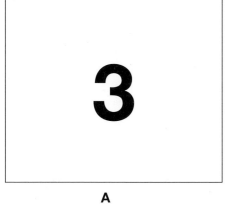

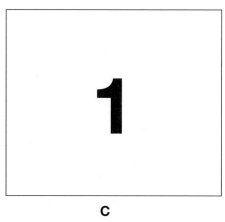

A   B   C

5 What time did Patrick say he would be home?

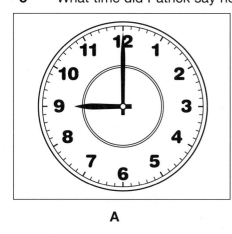

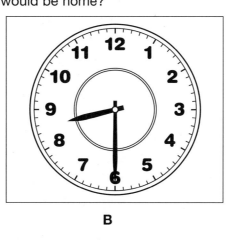

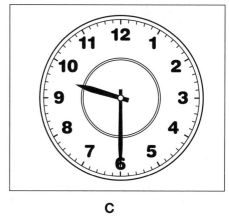

A   B   C

Part 2

Listen to Rita talking to a friend about her family's hobbies.
What hobby does each person have?
For questions **6–10**, write a letter **A–H** next to each person.
You will hear the conversation twice.

Example:

0   Cousin $\boxed{\text{A}}$

PEOPLE				**HOBBIES**	
6	Sister	☐		**A**	collecting stamps
7	Brother	☐		**B**	cycling
8	Mum	☐		**C**	fishing
9	Dad	☐		**D**	football
10	Granddad	☐		**E**	golf
				F	skiing
				G	swimming
				H	tennis

> **Exam tip**
> You will hear Rita's relatives mentioned in the same order as the questions. When you hear her mention a relative, you need to listen carefully to what she says about them. Then you need to match them to a hobby. Rita may mention more than one hobby for each relative but only one is correct.

Part 3

Questions 11–15

Listen to Ruben talking to a friend about something new he wants to buy.
For each question, choose the right answer (**A**, **B**, or **C**).
You will hear the conversation twice.

Example:

0   Ruben is going to buy a
  Ⓐ   laptop.
  B   desktop computer.
  C   mobile phone.

---

11   He is going to buy it from
  A   Computer Warehouse.
  B   the supermarket.
  C   Frank's Computers.

12   The shop is on
  A   Elizabeth Street.
  B   Mersey Road.
  C   Mary Street.

13   How much is it going to cost?
  A   £500
  B   £550
  C   £600

14   His mum will pick it up
  A   on Saturday.
  B   tonight.
  C   on Friday night.

15   On Saturday, Ruben's friend will visit him at
  A   10 o'clock.
  B   11 o'clock.
  C   1 o'clock.

> **Exam tip**   *The questions in a multiple-choice activity will give you information about what you will hear. You have 20 seconds to read them carefully before the conversation begins. Try to guess what the conversation will be about.*

Questions 16–20

You will hear a girl asking about music lessons.
Listen and complete each question.
You will hear the conversation twice.

Music lessons

Instrument: *piano*

Day: **(16)** ....

Time: **(17)** ....

Price per lesson: **(18)** £ ....

Address of music school: **(19)** ....

Teacher's mobile number: **(20)** ....

Exam tip	*Make sure you read the information in front of the gap carefully. Try to guess what type of information is missing before you listen. This will help you know what to listen out for.*

Part 5

You will hear some information about a play.
Listen and complete each question.
You will hear the information twice.

Play

Name: *The Princess and the Frog*

Days: **(21)** .... *and Sunday*

Play starts at: **(22)** ....

Be at theatre at: **(23)** ....

Price for children: **(24)** ....

To book tickets, call: **(25)** ....

Exam tip   *When you have to write a word, time, number or date in a box, write exactly what you hear. After listening, make any changes necessary so that your answer is clear. Remember spelling is important in this part.*

Part 1

In class

Work in pairs. Take turns to ask and answer these questions.

1   What subject is the easiest at school? Why?

2   When do you do your homework? Why?

3   What food do you like best? Why?

4   Have you been to any other towns in your country? Which ones?

5   Tell me something about your home town.

6   Tell me something about your family.

At home

Answer the questions on your own. You might want to record yourself so that you can play it back and hear yourself speak. What did you do well? What do you need to work on?

Exam tip	*If you don't understand a question, ask the examiner to repeat it. When answering, extend your answers a little – say more than just one word, especially with the questions beginning with 'Tell me something about ...'.*

Candidate A

A, here is some information about **a birthday party**. (Turn to page 140.)

B, you don't know anything about **the birthday party**, so ask **A** some questions about it.

Birthday Party
- name/boy?
- when/party?
- time/party?
- phone number?
- address?

Candidate B

B, here is some information about a bookshop. (Turn to page 142.)

A, you don't know anything about the bookshop, so ask **B** some questions about it.

Bookshop
- name/bookshop?
- open/Sunday?
- time/open?
- sell/schoolbooks?
- phone number?

> **Exam tip**
>
> *If you don't understand your partner's question, ask him/her to clarify or to repeat it. If you don't know what question to ask, think about the question and how it connects to the context (e.g. Is it a bookshop? Is it a music school? Is it a party?).*

Test 3

Part 1

Questions 1–5

Which notice (**A–H**) says this (**1–5**)?
For questions **1–5**, mark the correct letter **A–H** on your answer sheet.

Example:

0   You must bring these back when you finish.   *Answer:*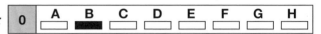

---

1   You must not do this here.

> **A**   NO RUNNING BY THE POOL.

2   You can't visit this place on this day.

> **B**   **Please return all sports equipment where you found it.**

3   These students do not have sports practice.

> **C**   *Swimming team*
> *No swimming training today.*
> *Ms Sharp is ill.*

4   You can't have this with you in this place.

> **D**   *No bags in the library, please. Leave them at the front desk.*

5   Call this number if you have lost something.

> **E**   **Year 7 camping trip**
> **Bus leaves Friday at 8.00 a.m.**
> **Don't be late!**

> **F**   **For more information,**
> **call 987 6543**

> **G**   *Found*
> *Small white dog with pink collar.*
> *Phone Trish on 87530980*

> **H**   **Museum opening times**
> **Tues–Sun 10–5.00**
> **Monday closed.**

Part 2

Read the sentences about a school trip.
Choose the best word (**A**, **B** or **C**) for each space.
For questions **6–10**, mark **A**, **B** or **C** on your answer sheet.

Example:

0   John's class .... on a school trip last Friday.

     A went   **B** came   **C** left

Answer:

0	A	B	C
	▬	☐	☐

---

6   The teacher .... them they would visit a local museum.

     A told   **B** said   **C** decided

7   They .... early in the morning from school.

     A took   **B** left   **C** passed

8   They spent the .... day at the museum and got back at 4.00.

     A whole   **B** most   **C** all

9   There were many things to see and John .... some postcards.

     A had   **B** took   **C** bought

10   He will .... one to his friend in America.

     A get   **B** send   **C** choose

Part 3

Complete the five conversations.
For questions **11–15**, mark **A**, **B** or **C** on your answer sheet.

Example:

0

Where do you live?

A in Hope Street.

B in my bedroom.

C in my house.

Answer: | 0 | A ▬ | B ☐ | C ☐ |

---

11 Can I have an orange juice, please?

    A No, I can't.

    B Here you are.

    C I'm thirsty.

12 I love your new shoes.

    A They're mine.

    B You're welcome.

    C Thanks.

13 I'm sorry, we don't have it in blue.

    A What a pity!

    B I agree.

    C I'll take it.

14 It's too loud.

    A I'll turn it down.

    B I'll turn it up.

    C I'll turn it on.

15 See you next week.

    A That's all right.

    B I can't see.

    C I can't wait!

Part 3

Complete the phone conversation between two friends.
What does Pat say to Pete?
For questions **16–20**, mark the correct letter **A–H** on your answer sheet.

Example:

Pete: Pat, it's me, Pete. I'm phoning to see if you're all right.

Pat: **0** ....A..............

Answer:

0	A	B	C	D	E	F	G	H
	■	☐	☐	☐	☐	☐	☐	☐

Pete: Will you be at school tomorrow?

Pat: **16** ....

Pete: Great! You haven't missed much at school.

Pat: **17** ....

Pete: We've got a school test to study for on Monday. I can tell you about it tomorrow.

Pat: **18** ....

Pete: No, actually, it's for maths.

Pat: **19** ....

Pete: I know. Mr Bryce decided to give us another one.

Pat: **20** ....

Pete: I'm sure he'll explain it all to you. Don't worry about it.

A	Hi. Thanks for asking. I'm feeling much better.
B	Is it for English?
C	That's good. I was worried about all the work I would have to do.
D	I haven't studied at all.
E	I won't be at school on Monday.
F	I hope so. I don't want to stay at home another day.
G	Really? But we just had one.
H	Wonderful! Will I be able to do it?

Questions 21–27

Read the article about a holiday.
Are sentences **21–27** Right' (**A**) or 'Wrong' (**B**)?
If there is not enough information to answer 'Right' (**A**) or 'Wrong' (**B**), choose 'Doesn't say' (**C**).
For questions **21–27**, mark **A**, **B** or **C** on your answer sheet.

A holiday to remember
By Sam Best

Last month my family and I went on our summer holiday. We usually go somewhere by the sea and spend our days swimming or just lying on the beach. We didn't do that this year. This year my parents took us to Disneyland Paris. We couldn't believe our luck when my sister and I found out that we would be spending five whole days visiting our dream theme park! We had never been to a theme park before and weren't too sure what to expect but it was an amazing experience.

On the first day, we visited the main park and went on a few rides. My favourite was the one called Big Thunder Mountain. It was like travelling on a small train in the mountains but a lot more exciting. But not all the rides were that good. For example, Snow White and the Seven Dwarfs was a little boring. We waited in a queue for a whole hour to get tickets for this ride and in the end we didn't really enjoy it. The next day we went to the Walt Disney Studios, where a guide gave us a tour. It was really interesting and we learnt a lot about how films and cartoons are made. We even 'met' some of the Disney characters!

The rest of the time we spent enjoying everything the park had to offer. Would I recommend Disneyland Paris? I would have to say, yes, with all my heart.

0   This year Sam and his family didn't go to the beach on their holiday.

A Right   **B** Wrong   **C** Doesn't say   *Answer:* | 0 | A ▬ | B ☐ | C ☐ |

---

21   Sam and his sister didn't really want to go to Disneyland Paris.

A Right   **B** Wrong   **C** Doesn't say

22   Every year their summer holiday is five days long.

A Right   **B** Wrong   **C** Doesn't say

23   Sam says Big Thunder Mountain was the best ride.

A Right   **B** Wrong   **C** Doesn't say

24   Only Sam enjoyed the Snow White ride.

A Right   **B** Wrong   **C** Doesn't say

25   Someone showed them the Walt Disney Studios.

A Right   **B** Wrong   **C** Doesn't say

26   At Walt Disney Studios they learnt something new.

A Right   **B** Wrong   **C** Doesn't say

27   Sam and his family will visit the park again next year.

A Right   **B** Wrong   **C** Doesn't say

Part 5

Read the article about life before mobile phones.
Choose the best word (**A**, **B** or **C**) for each space.
For questions **28–35**, mark **A**, **B** or **C** on your answer sheet.

Life before mobile phones

Many teenagers today cannot imagine what **(0)** .... parents did without mobile phones when they were young. But the idea of a mobile phone **(28)** .... not even enter their heads. Young people twenty years ago communicated with their friends **(29)** .... phone. They actually saw their friends and did things with them. In fact, they saw their friends **(30)** .... than most teenagers see their friends today. Young people read books, **(31)** .... TV and played with **(32)** .... young people. **(33)** .... they went out, their parents did not call them to see where they were. They had already been told where their children would **(34)** .... If they were on the bus, they did not send messages to their friends. They looked out of the window or they read a book. That's **(35)** .... young people did before mobile phones.

Example:

0	**A** them	**B** they	**C** their	*Answer:*	0	A ☐	B ☐	C ■

28	**A** had	**B** did	**C** were

29	**A** with	**B** by	**C** on

30	**A** much	**B** most	**C** more

31	**A** watched	**B** watch	**C** watching

32	**A** another	**B** other	**C** their

33	**A** If	**B** So	**C** As

34	**A** being	**B** be	**C** been

35	**A** where	**B** when	**C** what

Part 6

Read the descriptions of some words about the free time that people have.
What is the word for each one?
The first letter is already there. There is one space for each other letter in the word.
For questions **36–40**, write the words on your answer sheet.

Example:

0   This is where you can see interesting old things.   m _ _ _ _ _

Answer: | **0** | museum

---

36   This is where you stay on holiday when you sleep in a tent.   c _ _ _ _ _ _ _

37   If you want to read about music or fashion you might buy this.   m _ _ _ _ _ _ _

38   You do this when you become a member of a club.   j _ _ _

39   You use a camera to take this.   p _ _ _ _ _ _ _ _ _

40   This is what you do as a free-time activity.   h _ _ _ _ _

Questions 41–50

Complete the Internet message a young girl has written.
Write ONE word for each space.
For questions **41–50**, write the words on your answer sheet.

Example: | **0** | *is* |

My name **(0)** .... Katerina and I am 14 years **(41)** .... I am in Year 8 in

high school and my favourite subject is history. **(42)** .... my free time, I enjoy watching

films and going **(43)** .... with my friends. I have many interests but **(44)** ....

main interest is swimming. I am in a swimming team **(45)** .... I train three times

(46) .... week. I have **(47)** .... lucky enough to take part in many

competitions and have even visited other countries to compete. Just last month I **(48)** ....

to New Zealand with the team! I **(49)** .... really like music. My favourite singer is

Beyoncé. I love dancing along to **(50)** .... songs. She's great.

Questions 51–55

Read the advertisement and the email.
Fill in the information in the order form.
For questions **51–55**, write the information on your answer sheet.

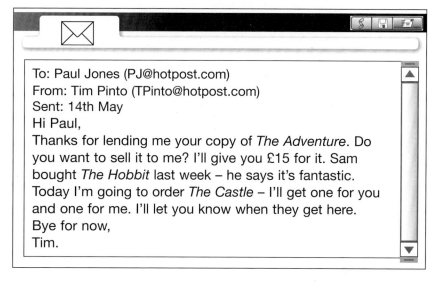

Games on sale

The Adventure – £20.99
The Hobbit – £17.99
The Castle – £25

To: Paul Jones (PJ@hotpost.com)
From: Tim Pinto (TPinto@hotpost.com)
Sent: 14th May
Hi Paul,
Thanks for lending me your copy of *The Adventure*. Do you want to sell it to me? I'll give you £15 for it. Sam bought *The Hobbit* last week – he says it's fantastic. Today I'm going to order *The Castle* – I'll get one for you and one for me. I'll let you know when they get here.
Bye for now,
Tim.

Order form

Customer:	*Tim Pinto*
Email address:	**51**
Name of game:	**52**
Date of order:	**53** *t*
Number of copies:	**54**
Total price:	**55**

Question 56

Read this email message from your friend Terry.

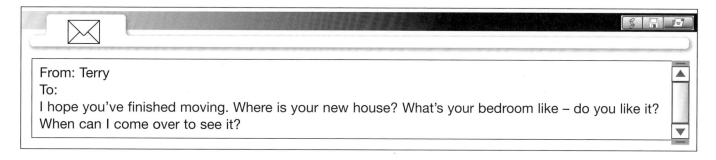

From: Terry
To:
I hope you've finished moving. Where is your new house? What's your bedroom like – do you like it? When can I come over to see it?

Write an email to Terry and answer the questions.
Write **25–35** words.
Write the email on your answer sheet.

Part 1

Questions 1–5

You will hear five short conversations.
You will hear each conversation twice.
There is one question for each conversation.
For each question, choose the right answer (**A**, **B** or **C**).

Example:　How long is the boy's project?

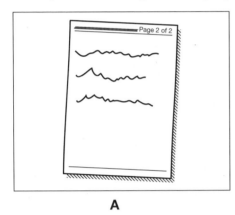

A

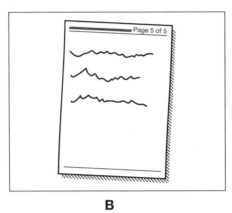

B

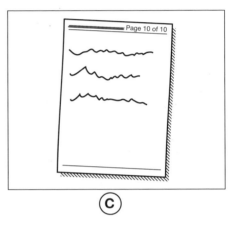

C

1　Which item of clothing does the woman decide to buy?

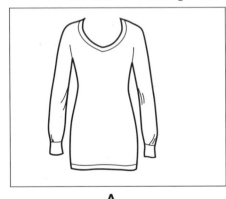

A

B

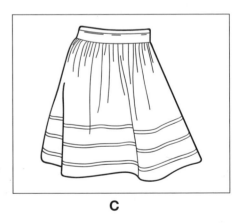

C

2　How far is the boy going to ride?

A

B

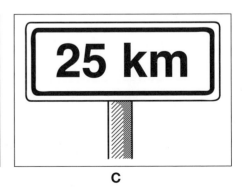

C

3 What time will the girl leave home?

A

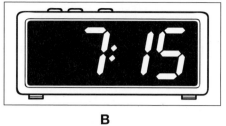

B

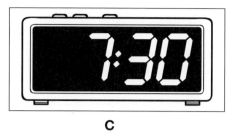

C

4 Where is the woman taking her family on holiday this year?

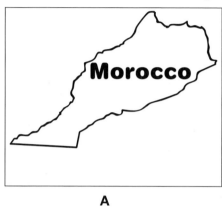

A

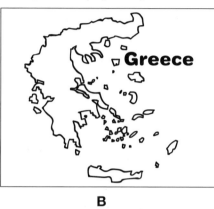

B

C

5 Which picture can the girl see?

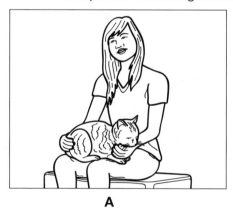

A

B

C

Part 2

Listen to Gus talking to his mum about his brothers and sisters.
What is each person doing?
For questions **6–10**, write a letter **A–H** next to each person.
You will hear the conversation twice.

Example:

Gus   **D**

PEOPLE			**ACTIVITIES**	
6	Penny	☐	A	bathing
7	Helen	☐	B	dressing
8	Paul	☐	C	on the computer
9	Tim	☐	D	on the phone
10	Ashley	☐	E	playing outside
			F	reading
			G	visiting a friend
			H	watching TV

Part 3

Listen to Nick talking to a shop assistant about two things he wants to buy.
For each question, choose the right answer (**A**, **B** or **C**).
You will hear the conversation twice.

Example:

0   What is the name of the book Nick wants to buy?

    A *The Island*

    B *The Treasure*

    C *Treasure Island*

---

11   The shop assistant sold the last copy of the book

    A this afternoon.

    B this morning.

    C a minute ago.

12   The shop assistant tells Nick to come in tomorrow

    A morning.

    B afternoon.

    C evening.

13   How much does the book cost?

    A £1

    B £5.50

    C £6.50

14   When can Nick pay for the book?

    A Tomorrow afternoon.

    B Tomorrow morning.

    C Now.

15   Nick's mum wants Nick to buy her a

    A cookbook.

    B cooking magazine.

    C a cooking DVD.

Part 4

You will hear a girl asking about tickets to a concert.
Listen and complete each question.
You will hear the conversation twice.

Concert

Bands:	Pink Elephant and Dragon
Day and date:	**(16)** .... 9th May
Starting time:	**(17)** ....
Number of tickets:	**(18)** £ ....
Name:	**(19)** Pat ....
Price per ticket:	**(20)** ....

Questions 21–25

You will hear some information about a museum.
Listen and complete each question.
You will hear the information twice.

<u>**Museum**</u>

Name: Bay City

Ground floor
    Left: **(21)** ....

    Right: **(22)** ....

First floor   various exhibits

                   (23) .... next to the lift

Second floor   **(24)** ....

                   views of the city

Guidebook
    Price: **(25)** £ ....

Test 3

Part 1

In class

Work in pairs. Take turns to ask and answer these questions.

1   Do you like your school? Why/Why not?

2   How many brothers and sisters have you got?

3   What do the members of your family do in their free time?

4   Can anyone else in your family speak English?

5   Tell me something about your home.

6   Tell me about a place you go to with your friends.

At home

Answer the questions on your own. You might want to record yourself so that you can play it back and hear yourself speak. What did you do well? What do you need to work on?

Part 2

Candidate A

A, here is some information about **an art museum**. (Turn to page 140.)

B, you don't know anything about **the art museum**, so ask **A** some questions about it.

Art Museum

- what/see?

- open/Monday?

- student ticket? cost?

- car park?

- address?

Candidate B

B, here is some information about **a bike race**. (Turn to page 142.)

A, you don't know anything about **the bike race**, so ask **B** some questions about it.

Bike race

- where?

- when?

- for children?

- website?

- what/win?

PAPER 1 Reading and Writing
(1 hour 10 minutes)

Part 1

Questions 1–5

Which notice (**A–H**) says this (**1–5**)?
For questions **1–5**, mark the correct letter **A–H** on your answer sheet.

Example:

0   You must not put your hand on this.   *Answer:* | 0 | A | B | C | D | E | F | G | H |

---

1   You must not do these things here.

2   Call this person if you want to buy this.

3   You can come here on any day to play this.

4   There is nobody here now.

5   Come here on this day if you want to do this.

A   NO SKATEBOARDING OR CYCLING IN THE PLAYGROUND.

B   **Do not touch.**

C   *Year 7 art exhibition*
     at the school auditorium all week

D   *Interested in being in the school play?*
     Come to room 3C after school on Friday.

E   **Skateboard for sale.**
     Almost new.
     Call Bob 5678900

F   **Indoor football centre**
     Open 7 days a week.

G   **Back in 20 minutes.**

H   THE SINGERS LIVE IN CONCERT
     TICKETS ON SALE NOW
     WWW.CONCERTTICKETS.COM

Part 2

Read the sentences about a sports team.
Choose the best word (**A**, **B** or **C**) for each space.
For questions **6–10**, mark **A, B** or **C** on your answer sheet.

Example:

0 Our football team .... the grand final last month.

    A won   **B** got   **C** had

Answer:

0	A	B	C
	▬	☐	☐

---

6 Our team is .... The Strikers.

    A said   **B** called   **C** known

7 I have been .... for The Strikers for two years now.

    A joining   **B** doing   **C** playing

8 We are a very good team but we sometimes .... a match.

    A take   **B** win   **C** lose

9 I have learnt a lot of .... playing for my team.

    A ways   **B** things   **C** kinds

10 It is .... to always do your best.

    A special   **B** useful   **C** important

Part 3

Complete the five conversations.

For questions **11–15**, mark **A**, **B** or **C** on your answer sheet.

Example:

0

How are you?

A Fine, thanks.

B It's very good.

C I'm here now.

Answer: | 0 | A | B | C |

---

11 Are you hungry?

    A No, I can't.

    B I've just eaten.

    C I can cook.

12 Would you like to come to my party?

    A Thank you.

    B I'm certain.

    C I'd love to.

13 Is your bike yellow?

    A Yes, I am.

    B No, it doesn't.

    C Yes, it is.

14 We won the match!

    A Congratulations!

    B Thank you.

    C I hope so.

15 Can you swim?

    A I'm not sure.

    B Of course I can.

    C I can't do that.

Part 3

Complete the conversation between a father and his daughter.
What does Helen say to her father?
For questions **16–20**, mark the correct letter **A–H** on your answer sheet.

Example:

Father: Helen, can you clean up your room, please?

Helen: **0** .... H ....   *Answer:*

0	A	B	C	D	E	F	G	H
	▭	▭	▭	▭	▭	▭	▭	▬

Father: It doesn't look like it to me.

Helen: **16** ....

Father: Well, you'll need to find some time to do some work around the house too.

Helen: **17** ....

Father: But that's what you always say and then it never gets done!

Helen: **18** ....

Father: All right. But if you don't do it tomorrow, I'll take the computer out of your room.

Helen: **19** ....

Father: I know you do but you spend too much time on it and not enough time helping out around the home.

Helen: **20** ....

Father: I hope so, Helen. You need to learn that we can't always do everything for you.

A I know you think I'm on the Internet again but I'm actually working.

B I've got a project to finish tonight, so please let me do it.

C I'll change. I'll start cleaning my room and helping you and Mum more.

D I'm answering some emails.

E I don't like cleaning my room.

F You can't do that! I need it.

G I'll do it tomorrow – really I will.

H But, Dad, can't you see I'm really busy?

Part 4

Read the article about using the Internet.
Are sentences **21–27** 'Right' (**A**) or 'Wrong' (**B**)?
If there is not enough information to answer 'Right' (**A**) or 'Wrong' (**B**), choose 'Doesn't say' (**C**).
For questions **21–27**, mark **A**, **B** or **C** on your answer sheet.

Is your computer safe?

By Sally West

Many people think that because they are the only ones using their computer, that their computer is safe. But is it? If you are connected to the Internet, the answer to this question is no, it is not. There are a lot of things your computer can catch from the Internet. For a start there are viruses. A virus is a piece of code that you download without knowing it from the Internet. This piece of code can copy itself and can cause very serious problems for your computer. For example, it can destroy all your files and important information you have on your computer.

Another unpleasant thing that can happen is that you get hundreds of spam emails every day. This can happen if you give your email address to people you don't know or to websites on the Internet. Giving your email to people you don't know can also put you in danger. You can be tricked into buying things or doing things that can hurt you. Certain bad people often try to find someone to trick. If they have your email address, they can send you a message that may contain false information.

So, if you are using the Internet, you need to be careful that you do not put yourself in any danger. Don't give out your name and email address to people you do not know and don't download things from websites you are not certain of. Use the Internet with care.

Example:

0   If you are the only person using your computer, your computer will be safe.

       A Right   **B** Wrong   **C** Doesn't say   *Answer:* | 0 | A ☐ | B ■ | C ☐ |

---

21   People download viruses every time they use the Internet.

       A Right   **B** Wrong   **C** Doesn't say

22   A virus is a piece of code that makes copies of itself.

       A Right   **B** Wrong   **C** Doesn't say

23   Spam email is email you don't want.

       A Right   **B** Wrong   **C** Doesn't say

24   You can get spam email even if you give your email address to your friends.

       A Right   **B** Wrong   **C** Doesn't say

25   Some bad people can send you false messages.

       A Right   **B** Wrong   **C** Doesn't say

26   If you are using the Internet, you are never safe.

       A Right   **B** Wrong   **C** Doesn't say

27   It is not a good idea to download songs from the Internet.

       A Right   **B** Wrong   **C** Doesn't say

Part 5

Read the article about someone's life when they were young.
Choose the best word (**A**, **B** or **C**) for each space.
For questions **28–35**, mark **A**, **B** or **C** on your answer sheet.

When I was young

As a child, I grew up (0) .... a big city. I enjoyed living in the
city – there was so (28) .... to do. My friends lived close
(29) .... me so we would meet each other after school and go
to the pool or just play games at one of our houses. The only time
I got to see the countryside (30) .... when we would go on
summer holiday with (31) .... parents.

   We sometimes went to the beach (32) .... a week or we
went to visit my cousins on their farm. It was strange to
(33) .... out of the city. I wasn't used to (34) .... so
much green or animals like cows or sheep. The only animals we saw in the city were birds, cats or
dogs. Now I live in a small country town and my life is very different. I miss the big city (35) I
don't think I would want to live there.

Example:

| **0** | **A** in | **B** at | **C** on | *Answer:* | **0** | A ▬ | B ☐ | C ☐ |

28	**A** far	**B** many	**C** much
29	**A** to	**B** in	**C** at
30	**A** is	**B** was	**C** were
31	**A** my	**B** mine	**C** me
32	**A** during	**B** since	**C** for
33	**A** be	**B** being	**C** been
34	**A** see	**B** seen	**C** seeing
35	**A** but	**B** and	**C** or

Part 6

Read the descriptions of some words about clothes and accessories.
What is the word for each one?
The first letter is already there. There is one space for each other letter in the word.
For questions **36–40**, write the words on your answer sheet.

Example:

0   You need this if it rains.   u _ _ _ _ _ _ _

Answer: | **0** | umbrella |

---

36   You wear this so that you know what time it is.   w _ _ _ _

37   This is where you put your money.   w _ _ _ _ _

38   You do this when you put your clothes on.   d _ _ _ _

39   You wear this so that you don't get wet when it's raining.   r _ _ _ _ _ _ _

40   You wear these on your feet when you play sport.   t _ _ _ _ _ _ _

Part 7

Complete the note from a mother to her son.
Write ONE word for each space.
For questions **41–50**, write the words on your answer sheet.

Example:

0	and

Sweetheart,

Peter called **(0)** .... wants you to call **(41)** .... back. He said he wants you to

(42) .... him what you **(43)** .... today at school. He said he won't

(44) .... able to make it to bowling tonight. Also, dinner is in **(45)** .... oven. Heat

it up and please put your plate in the dishwasher when you **(46)** .... finished. Could

(47) .... please take out the rubbish and pick up **(48)** .... milk from the

supermarket. I **(49)** .... be home after 7.00, so I'll **(50)** .... you then.

Love,

Mum

Part 8

Read the advertisement and email.
Complete Kelly's notes.
For questions **51–55**, write the information on your answer sheet.

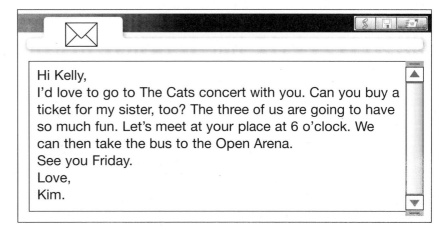

**The Cats
Live in Concert**

Friday February 14th 7.30pm.
Open Arena
Tickets on sale from Ticketof-
fice.com
Adults: £20   Students: £10

Hi Kelly,
I'd love to go to The Cats concert with you. Can you buy a ticket for my sister, too? The three of us are going to have so much fun. Let's meet at your place at 6 o'clock. We can then take the bus to the Open Arena.
See you Friday.
Love,
Kim.

Kelly's notes

Name of band:	*The Cats*
Concert date:	**51**
Time:	**52**
Meet Kim at my place at:	**53**
Total price of tickets:	**54**
Go to the concert by:	**55**

Part 9

Question 56

Read this email message from your friend Louise.

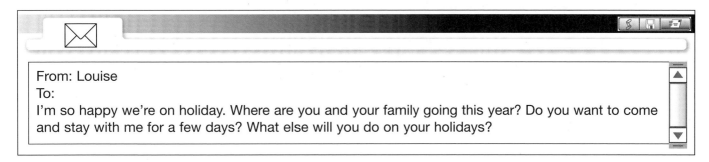

From: Louise
To:
I'm so happy we're on holiday. Where are you and your family going this year? Do you want to come and stay with me for a few days? What else will you do on your holidays?

Write an email to Louise and answer the questions.

Write **25–35** words.

Write the email on your answer sheet.

Part 1

Questions 1–5

You will hear five short conversations.
You will hear each conversation twice.
There is one question for each conversation.
For each question, choose the right answer (**A**, **B** or **C**).

Example: What time does the film actually start?

A   B   C

1   Which animal did the boy see on the safari?

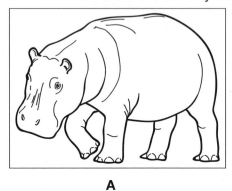 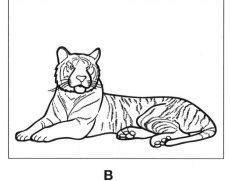 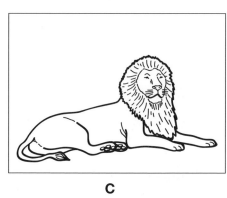

A   B   C

2   Which bus stop should the girl get off the bus at?

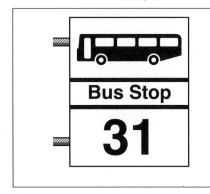 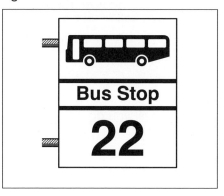 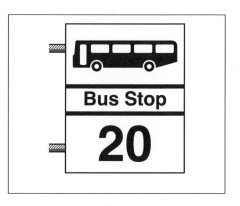

A   B   C

3 Which part or parts of her body has Pam hurt?

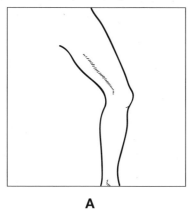

A

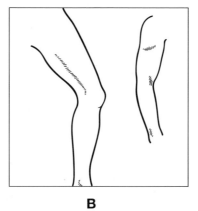

B

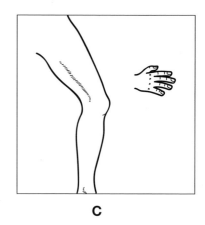

C

4 What was the weather like yesterday?

A

B

C

5 What does the man want the boy to buy him?

A

B

C

Part 2

Listen to Irene talking to her friend about her family's reading habits.
What does each person in her family like to read?
For questions **6–10**, write a letter **A–H** next to each person.
You will hear the conversation twice.

Example:

0	Irene	H

PEOPLE

6 Grandma ☐

7 Dad ☐

8 Mum ☐

9 Brother ☐

10 Sister ☐

ACTIVITIES

A books

B diaries

C emails

D letters

E magazines

F menus

G newspapers

H postcards

Part 3

Listen to Marie talking to her friend about how she spent her weekend.
For each question, choose the right answer (**A**, **B** or **C**).
You will hear the conversation twice.

Example:

0   Marie's cousins are visiting from

Ⓐ   Ireland.

B   Scotland.

C   England.

---

11   Where did they go on Friday night?

A   shopping

B   a restaurant

C   the zoo

12   On Saturday, they went to the cinema at

A   5.00.

B   6.00.

C   7.00.

13   Which film did they go to see?

A   *Rock Star*

B   *Star Trek*

C   *Star Wars*

14   Marie didn't see the film because her cousins were

A   talking.

B   laughing.

C   eating.

15   Marie's cousins left on

A   Sunday night.

B   Monday morning.

C   Monday afternoon.

Part 4

Questions 16–20

You will hear a girl talking to her coach.
Listen and complete each question.
You will hear the conversation twice.

Volleyball practice

Day: Friday

Date: **(16)** .... June

Place: **(17)** Smith ....

Time: **(18)** 5.00 – ....

Form must be signed by: **(19)** ....

Coach's phone number: **(20)** ....

Part 5

You will hear some information about a film festival for young people.
Listen and complete each question.
You will hear the information twice.

Teen Film Festival

Dates:	25–26 March
For tickets call:	**(21)** ....
Price of tickets:	£10 for adults;
	(22) .... for students and children
Competition for tickets:	
Send message to:	**(23)** ....
Write your name and	**(24)** ....
You will know if you have won next **(25)**	

Part 1

In class

Work in pairs. Take turns to ask and answer these questions.

1   What's your surname? How do you spell that?

2   Where do you live? How long have you lived there?

3   What do you think of your home town? Why?

4   In your town, where do people go at weekends?

5   Tell me something about another town or place in your country.

6   Tell me something about your room.

At home

Answer the questions on your own. You might want to record yourself so that you can play it back and hear yourself speak. What did you do well? What do you need to work on?

Part 2

Candidate A

A, here is some information about **an animal hospital**. (Turn to page 141.)

B, you don't know anything about **the animal hospital**, so ask **A** some questions about it.

Animal hospital

- name/animal hospital?

- open/Saturday?

- for horses?

- car park?

- address?

Candidate B

B, here is some information about **tennis lessons**. (Turn to page 143.)

A, you don't know anything about **the tennis lessons**, so ask **B** some questions about them.

Tennis Lessons

- where?

- expensive?

- need/tennis racket?

- lessons/Sunday?

- phone number?

Part 1

Questions 1–5

Which notice (**A–H**) says this (**1–5**)?
For questions **1–5**, mark the correct letter **A–H** on your answer sheet.

Example:

0   Come to this place before you use this.   *Answer:* | 0 | A | B | C | D | E | F | G | H |

---

1   You can buy this almost new.

2   You should do this before you enter here.

3   You must not cross here before it is time.

4   You can travel to this place all day.

5   This place is not open every day.

A
> **London – Brighton.**
> **Buses every hour on the hour.**
> **07.00 – 22.00**

B
> **Keep your classroom clean.**
> **Please put your rubbish**
> **in the bin.**

C
> *Science museum*
> *Open 10am – 5.00pm*
> *Closed Tuesday*
> *Adults: £5*
> *Students and children: free*

D
> **Please shower before using the pool.**

E
> FOR SALE
> BOYZONE VIDEO GAME
> ONLY PLAYED ONCE
> £10
> PHONE 9368769

F
> **No tickets left for tonight's concert.**

G
> *Want to use a computer?*
> *Please book time at the front desk.*

H
> **Wait behind the yellow line.**

Part 2

Read the sentences about a holiday place.
Choose the best word (**A**, **B** or **C**) for each space.
For questions **6–10**, mark **A**, **B** or **C** on your answer sheet.

Example:

0   My family and I have a beach holiday .... summer.

    A every   **B** the   **C** all

Answer:

0	A	B	C
	■	☐	☐

---

6   My sister and I spend .... of the day swimming at the beach.

    A each   **B** more   **C** most

7   My mum .... sunbathing and reading a book.

    A enjoys   **B** goes   **C** does

8   My father doesn't like sitting in the sun so he lies .... an umbrella.

    A over   **B** under   **C** next

9   Next summer we would .... to go a Greek island for our summer holiday.

    A like   **B** want   **C** enjoy

10   I have never been to Greece before and I can't .... to go.

    A stay   **B** wait   **C** stop

Part 3

Complete the five conversations.
For questions **11–15**, mark **A**, **B** or **C** on your answer sheet.

Example:

0

Answer:

0	A	B	C

---

11 Did you see the match last night?

    A Of course!

    B I agree!

    C No, I haven't.

12 Did you go cycling on Sunday?

    A I'd love to.

    B Yes, I did.

    C No, I don't.

13 Who was that on the phone?

    A Just a friend.

    B Yes, it was.

    C I didn't hear it.

14 What's the date today?

    A It's the 25th.

    B It's 2012.

    C It's Thursday.

15 Where did you put my laptop?

    A On your desk.

    B I didn't want it.

    C I really like it.

Complete the conversation between two friends.
What does Andrew say to Sarah?
For questions **16–20**, mark the correct letter **A–H** on your answer sheet.

Example:

Sarah: How was the party on Saturday?

Andrew: **0** ....H............

Answer:

0	A	B	C	D	E	F	G	H
								■

Sarah: Yes, I really wanted to go but I had to go to a wedding with my parents.

Andrew: **16** ....

Sarah: Really boring. I'm sure the party was a lot more fun.

Andrew: **17** ....

Sarah: Who was there? Was Cliff there?

Andrew: **18** ....

Sarah: Really? I wonder why.

Andrew: **19** ....

Sarah: Everyone except for me. What did you get Sharon?

Andrew: **20** ....

Sarah: Oh, I'm sure she loved that.

A   What was that like?

B   No. I thought he would be but he didn't come.

C   No, I didn't enjoy it at all.

D   Yes, I'm sure it was.

E   I'm not sure, I'm thinking of getting her some flowers.

F   I got her a CD. The Flowers' new one.

G   Everyone from school was there though.

H   It was great. It's a pity you couldn't be there.

Questions 21–27

Read the article about three teenagers' hobbies.
For questions **21–27**, mark **A**, **B** or **C** on your answer sheet.

What's your hobby?

Most people collect things and I'm no exception. I've been collecting posters since I was 9 years old. I'm now 14, so you can imagine how many posters I've got! I've got all sorts – from small ones I've found in magazines to very large ones I've bought at concerts or sporting events. My favourite poster is one that I have of my favourite film – *The Lord of the Rings*. It's more than a metre high and I've put it up on my bedroom wall where I can see it when I'm lying in bed.

My hobby is my music. I sing and play the drums in an all-girl group. We started the group only last year, but we have already played five concerts – two of them at school! Many people ask me how can I sing when I'm playing the drums. I don't think it's at all difficult. Of course I'm not the only singer in the group. Melissa, one of the guitarists, also sings. I really love my hobby and hope that when I grow up I will be in a famous band.

I've always been a very sporty person and living where I do, in Norway, the natural thing to do was a snow sport. Every winter I go snowboarding with my father and my brother. It's a very exciting sport and can be a little dangerous if you're not careful. I'd like to try skateboarding because people tell me it's a little like snowboarding. Maybe next year I will ask my parents to get me a skateboard for my birthday.

Example:

0   When did Bill start collecting posters?

A Five years ago.   **B** Last year.   **C** When he was 14 years old.

Answer: | 0 | A ▬ | B ☐ | C ☐ |

---

21   Bill says he's got posters

      A from all over the world.   **B** from magazines only.   **C** of all sizes.

22   The poster that Bill loves best is

      A on his bedroom wall.   **B** a small one.   **C** of his favourite group.

23   Lauren says her group has

      A never played in front of people.   **B** has played at school.   **C** got both boys and girls in it.

24   How many singers are in Lauren's band?

      A One.   **B** Two   **C** Five.

25   When she's older, Lauren says she would like to

      A stop playing in a band.   **B** start a new instrument.   **C** be a well-known musician.

26   Nathan goes snowboarding

      A only at weekends.   **B** with his family.   **C** all year round.

27   Nathan would like to start skateboarding because

      A he got a skateboard for his birthday   **B** it's like the hobby he has got now.   **C** he'd like to stop snowboarding.

Questions 28–35

Read the article about a teenager named Nettie.
Choose the best word (**A**, **B** or **C**) for each space.
For questions **28–35**, mark **A**, **B** or **C** on your answer sheet.

Nettie Polano

Nettie Polano is 14 years old but she does not go to school with other girls **(0)** .... age. She does not go to school **(28)** .... she is a university student. Nettie is a teenage genius – a teenager with amazing abilities. She completed primary school in four years and secondary school in only three!

She **(29)** .... decided to study science because she dreams of one day becoming the **(30)** .... person to travel into space. Her teachers noticed she was different from **(31)** .... students in her class **(32)** .... she was only 7 years old. They told Nettie's parents how brilliant she **(33)** .... and her parents took Nettie out of school when she was only 9 years old. Nettie completed her secondary education at home with teachers **(34)** .... tutored her on her own. They, too, noticed how brilliant Nettie was and encouraged her to study science at university.

(35) .... is she happy? Nettie says she is. She still sees her old school friends and she still does things other teenagers her age enjoy.

Example:

0	**A** her	**B** his	**C** its	*Answer:*	0	A ▆	B ☐	C ☐

28	**A** because	**B** so	**C** but
29	**A** has	**B** have	**C** had
30	**A** youngest	**B** young	**C** younger
31	**A** other	**B** another	**C** every
32	**A** where	**B** when	**C** why
33	**A** was	**B** is	**C** been
34	**A** who	**B** whose	**C** which
35	**A** Although	**B** And	**C** But

Part 6

Read the descriptions of some things that you can find at home.
What is the word for each one?
The first letter is already there. There is one space for each other letter in the word.
For questions **36–40**, write the words on your answer sheet.

Example:

0   This is a phone you can take with you.   m _ _ _ _ _

Answer: | **0** | *mobile* |

---

36   You put food and drinks in this to keep them cold.   f _ _ _ _ _

37   You use this to tell time.   c _ _ _ _

38   You can hear music on this.   r _ _ _ _

39   You can watch films and other things on this.   t _ _ _ _ _ _ _ _ _

40   You can put this on a table to give you light.   l _ _ _

Questions 41–50

Complete this postcard.
Write ONE word for each space.
For questions **41–50**, write the words on your answer sheet.

Example: | **0** | *the* |

Dear Jack,

I'm sitting on the beach at **(0)** .... moment.

I've just **(41)** .... swimming and soon I'm going to

(42) .... beach volleyball **(43)** .... my sister

and some friends. We are **(44)** .... a wonderful time.

It's beautiful here. The water **(45)** .... a little

cold but it doesn't matter because it's so hot outside.

We've **(46)** .... some really interesting places and

tomorrow we're **(47)** .... to spend the day walking

in the mountains. I've taken lots **(48)** .... photographs.

I'll show **(49)** .... them when I see you.

We **(50)** .... be back next week. I'll call you then.

Love,

Kim.

Part 8

Read the two notes about a school trip.
Complete Kim's notes.
For questions **51–55**, write the information on your answer sheet.

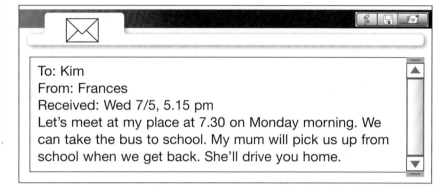

School trip to Cambridge

Monday 12th May

Leave from school at 8 am

Bring your own lunch

To: Kim
From: Frances
Received: Wed 7/5, 5.15 pm
Let's meet at my place at 7.30 on Monday morning. We can take the bus to school. My mum will pick us up from school when we get back. She'll drive you home.

Kim's notes

School trip:	Cambridge
Date:	**51**
Take:	**52**
Meet Frances at:	**53**
Get to school by:	**54**
Get home by:	**55**

Part 9

You have lost your new mobile phone. Write a notice to put on the wall at your school.

Say:

- **where** you lost your mobile phone.
- **what** your mobile phone looks like and **how** to return it to you.

Write **25–35** words.
Write the notice on your answer sheet.

Part 1

Questions 1–5

You will hear five short conversations.
You will hear each conversation twice.
There is one question for each conversation.
For each question, choose the right answer (**A**, **B** or **C**).

Example: Which is the girl's house?

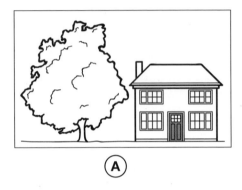

(A)

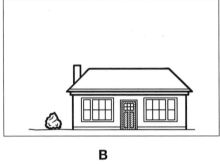

B

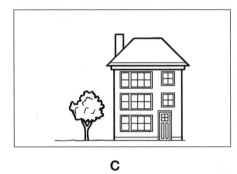

C

1   How much does the laptop cost?

A   **B**

C

2   What is the girl doing now?

A   **B**

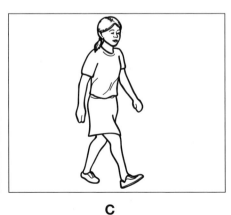

C

3 What time will the girl meet her teacher?

A

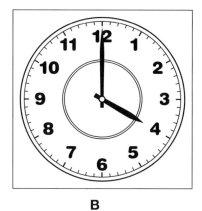

B

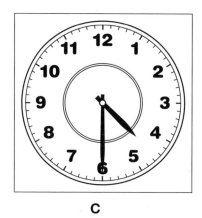

C

4 When is Tina's birthday?

Month						
M	**T**	**W**	**T**	**F**	**S**	**S**
			1	2	③	4
5	6	7	8	9	10	11
12	13	14	15	16	17	18
19	20	21	22	23	24	25
26	27	28	28	30	31	

A

Month						
M	**T**	**W**	**T**	**F**	**S**	**S**
			1	2	3	4
5	6	7	8	9	10	11
12	⑬	14	15	16	17	18
19	20	21	22	23	24	25
26	27	28	28	30	31	

B

Month						
M	**T**	**W**	**T**	**F**	**S**	**S**
			1	2	3	4
5	6	7	8	9	10	11
12	13	14	15	16	17	18
19	20	21	22	23	24	25
26	27	28	28	㉚	31	

C

5 Where are the speakers going at the weekend?

A

B

C

Part 2

Listen to Tim talking to a friend about a school camp.
What activities did he do each day?
For questions **6–10**, write a letter **A–H** next to each day.
You will hear the conversation twice.

Example:

0   Wednesday   ☐H

DAYS

6   Thursday   ☐

7   Friday   ☐

8   Saturday   ☐

9   Sunday   ☐

10   Monday   ☐

ACTIVITIES

A   fishing

B   guided tour

C   horse-riding

D   playing games

E   swimming

F   tennis

G   volleyball

H   walking

Part 3

Listen to Vivienne talking to her mother about buying a new computer game.
For each question, choose the right answer (**A**, **B** or **C**).
You will hear the conversation twice.

Example:

0   Who did Vivienne go shopping with?

    A   her mum

    B   Sharon

    (C)   Tammy

---

11   How many computer games does Vivienne now have?

    A   8

    B   9

    C   10

12   What's the name of her new computer game?

    A   *Fashion*

    B   *Fashion Week*

    C   *Designer*

13   How much did Vivienne pay for the game?

    A   £10

    B   £20

    C   £40

14   Where did Vivienne buy the game?

    A   Paul's

    B   John's Computers

    C   Small World

15   What else does the shop sell?

    A   computers

    B   films and music

    C   books

Part 4

You will hear Damien and Jenny talking about a party.
Listen and complete each question.
You will hear the conversation twice.

Damien's party

Damien will be: 14 years old

Day: (16) ....

Time: (17) ....

Place: (18) ....

Address: (19) .... Street

Get there by: (20) ....

Part 5

You will hear some information about Edinburgh Castle.
Listen and complete each question.
You will hear the information twice.

Edinburgh Castle

Guide's name:	Lisa Connery
Lang Stairs:	**(21)** .... steps to climb.
Entrance to castle:	**(22)** .... of the stairs.
Meeting point:	**(23)** on the ....
Entrance fee:	£11 adults,
	(24) .... children.
Guidebook costs:	**(25)** ....

Part 1

In class

Work in pairs. Take turns to ask and answer these questions.

1   What subjects are the most interesting at school? Why?

2   Do you live near here?

3   How did you travel to school today?

4   How long did it take?

5   Tell me something about your language school.

6   Tell me something about the area you live in.

At home

Answer the questions on your own. You might want to record yourself so that you can play it back and hear yourself speak. What did you do well? What do you need to work on?

Part 2

Candidate A

A, here is some information about **some photography classes**. (Turn to page 141.)

B, you don't know anything about **the photography classes**, so ask **A** some questions about them.

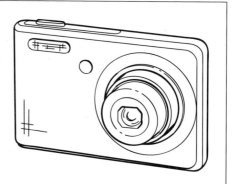

PHOTOGRAPHY CLASSES

- where/classes?

- when/classes?

- need/camera?

- phone number?

- cost?

Candidate B

B, here is some information about **a DVD club**. (Turn to page 143.)

A, you don't know anything about **the DVD club**, so ask **B** some questions about it.

DVD Club

- name/DVD club?

- where/DVD club?

- rent/games?

- open/Sundays?

- website?

Part 1

Questions 1–5

Which notice (**A–H**) says this (**1–5**)?
For questions **1–5,** mark the correct letter **A–H** on your answer sheet.

Example:

0 Send a message here if you want to learn to do this.

Answer:

0	A	B	C	D	E	F	G	H

1 You can call this number any time.

A

> LONDON TRAVEL INFORMATION
> 020 7222 0123
> 24 HOURS

2 You must not enter here.

B

> **I want to know what you thought of the lesson today. Complete the form and put it in the box.**

3 You should talk to this person if you want to join.

C

> *Groups (Mon–Fri only) £6*
> *Call the museum ticket office on*
> *020 7887 8899*

4 These students do not have to meet today.

D

> **Singing lessons**
> **Contact Samantha**
> samantha@sing.com

5 You can give your opinion if you do this.

E

> **PHOTOGRAPHY CLUB**
> **MEETS WED 4–6**
> **IF YOU'RE INTERESTED,**
> **SEE MS SHRIMPTON IN RM 4C**

F

> **Don't throw rubbish on the ground. Use the bins!**

G

> **Football team**
> **No practice today.**
> **Mr Peters is ill.**
> **H**

H

> **Please use other door**

Part 2

Read the sentences about a school.
Choose the best word (**A**, **B** or **C**) for each space.
For questions **6–10**, mark **A**, **B** or **C** on your answer sheet.

Example:

0 My school is in a .... old building in the centre of town.

   A lots   **B** very   **C** much

   Answer:

0	A	B	C
	☐	■	☐

---

6 The school is .... the road from the train station.

   A next   **B** across   **C** opposite

7 There are .... than a hundred students at the school.

   A only   **B** under   **C** fewer

8 Most people .... that the school is one of the most beautiful buildings in the town.

   A believe   **B** opinion   **C** tell

9 Every morning I go to school on .... but I come back home by bus.

   A leg   **B** walk   **C** foot

10 It .... me 10 minutes to walk to school.

   A takes   **B** gets   **C** has

Questions 11–15

Complete the five conversations.
For questions **11–15**, mark **A, B or C** on your answer sheet.

Example:

0

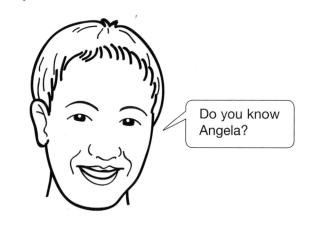

Do you know Angela?

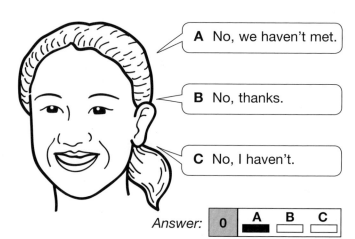

A No, we haven't met.

B No, thanks.

C No, I haven't.

Answer:

0	A	B	C
	■	☐	☐

---

11 Let's go home.

    A It's still early.

    B How long for?

    C It's all right.

12 May I use your phone?

    A Yes, you can.

    B Yes, it is.

    C Yes, of course.

13 Do you want to play a game?

    A That's a good idea.

    B Yes, I can.

    C Yes, I like it.

14 Who was that on the phone?

    A Jane's here.

    B Your dad.

    C Pam hasn't called.

15 They're not answering.

    A I hope so.

    B They're over there.

    C They must be out.

Part 3

Complete the conversation between a brother and sister.
What does Rita say to Peter?
For questions **16–20**, mark the correct letter **A–H** on your answer sheet.

Example:

Peter: Where have you been? We've been trying to call you.

Rita: **0** .... H ....

Answer:

Peter: Didn't you have your mobile with you?

Rita: **16** ....

Peter: We all tried to call you but you weren't answering.

Rita: **17** ....

Peter: No, they were just worried.

Rita: **18** ....

Peter: What film did you go and see?

Rita: **19** ....

Peter: Are you sure you were at the cinema?

Rita: **20** ....

Peter: Maybe because you were somewhere else.

A	I can't remember the name of it.
B	Yes, I did. It was great!
C	I did but I had it turned off.
D	I'll call them in a few minutes.
E	Of course! Why would I lie?
F	The film was very good.
G	Were Mum and Dad angry?
H	I was at the cinema. Why?

Read the article about a young boy called Thanasis.
For questions **21–27**, mark **A**, **B** or **C** on your answer sheet.

The English-speaking Waiter

Thanasis is 10 years old and lives in a small village on a beautiful Greek island. Like all children his age, Thanasis has just completed year 4 in primary school. But unlike other children his age, Thanasis also has a full-time job for two months of the year. In the busy summer months Thanasis is a waiter in his family's restaurant. In July and August, the restaurant is very popular with tourists from all over the world. Because he is the only person in his family who can speak English, it is his job to look after the tourists when they eat at the restaurant. He explains the menu, he takes their order and he even carries the heavy trays to their table.

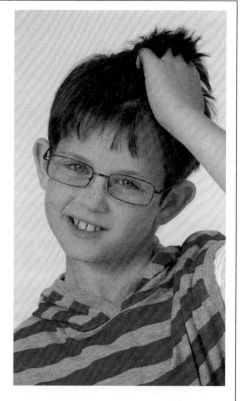

Where did he learn his English? There is no school in Thanasis' village, and during the school year he travels 12 kilometres every day by bus to a nearby village to go to school. Together with his classmates, two evenings a week, he attends English classes at a language school in the same village. There is no bus service when his classes end, so his mother picks him up and brings him home. Thanasis doesn't mind, he enjoys learning English. He is very pleased that he can help his family in the summer and the tourists are very happy that they can order their meal in English. What does Thanasis want to do when he grows up? He wants to own a restaurant, of course!

0 In the summer, the other children in Thanasis' village

A work full time. **B** go to school. **C** don't work. *Answer:*

---

21 The restaurant Thanasis works in

A belongs to his family. **B** is closed in the winter. **C** is not very busy.

22 Thanasis helps his family in the restaurant because he

A wants to be a waiter. **B** gets paid to. **C** can speak English.

23 Who does Thanasis serve at the restaurant?

A the tourists **B** the children **C** everybody

24 Where does Thanasis go to school?

A in his village **B** in another village. **C** in a nearby town

25 Where does he learn English?

A in a language school **B** in primary school **C** at home

26 Thanasis is very happy because

A he likes school. **B** he talks to many tourists. **C** he can help his family.

27 What job does Thanasis want to do when he's older?

A He wants to have **B** He wants to be **C** He wants to be a waiter.
his own restaurant.   an English teacher.

Part 5

Read the article about hip hop music.
Choose the best word (**A**, **B** or **C**) for each space.
For questions **28–35**, mark **A**, **B** or **C** on your answer sheet.

Hip Hop

Most people know hip hop as a style **(0)** .... music but in fact hip hop is more **(28)** .... just the music. It is the words, the dance and generally a whole culture of young people who sing it, dance it **(29)** .... live it.

   (30) .... began its history in the Bronx area of New York City as early as the 1970s. But hip hop music **(31)** .... not start from nothing. Like all music, it had its beginnings in another kind of music. In the case of hip hop, this music **(32)** .... African American music, and some even say African music. **(33)** .... the 1990s hip hop has also become very popular in other parts of the world. For example. in Europe, Africa and Asia it is the **(34)** .... popular style of music for teenagers. Hip hop has already been around for almost 40 years. Like rock and roll, it **(35)** .... probably be around for at least another 40.

Example:

| 0 | **A** at | **B** from | **C** of | *Answer:* | 0 | A ☐ | B ☐ | C ▅ |

28	**A** as	**B** that	**C** than
29	**A** and	**B** so	**C** but
30	**A** There	**B** That	**C** It
31	**A** did	**B** was	**C** had
32	**A** be	**B** was	**C** being
33	**A** Since	**B** From	**C** For
34	**A** more	**B** most	**C** best
35	**A** will	**B** is	**C** must

Part 6

Read the descriptions of words about reading and writing.
What is the word for each one?
The first letter is already there. There is one space for each other letter in the word.
For questions **36–40**, write the words on your answer sheet.

Example:

0   You send this to someone when you're on holiday.   p _ _ _ _ _ _ _

Answer: | **0** | *postcard* |

---

36   This is a letter you write on the computer.   e _ _ _ _ _

37   You do this when you send a message from your mobile.   t _ _ _

38   You can read about what happens in the world in this.   n _ _ _ _ _ _ _ _

39   This is where you write your appointments.   d _ _ _ _ _

40   You can give someone this on their birthday.   c _ _ _ _

Part 7

Complete these emails.
Write ONE word for each space.
For questions **41–50**, write the words on your answer sheet.

Example: | 0 | was |

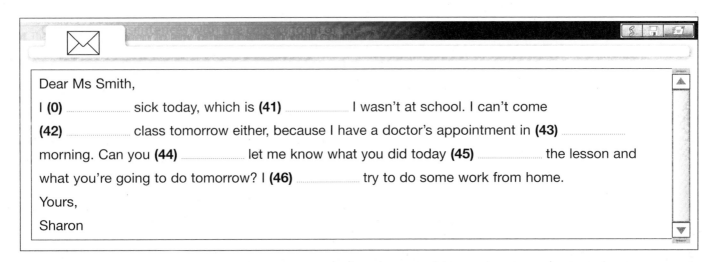

Dear Ms Smith,

I **(0)** .... sick today, which is **(41)** .... I wasn't at school. I can't come

(42) .... class tomorrow either, because I have a doctor's appointment in **(43)** ....

morning. Can you **(44)** .... let me know what you did today **(45)** .... the lesson and

what you're going to do tomorrow? I **(46)** .... try to do some work from home.

Yours,

Sharon

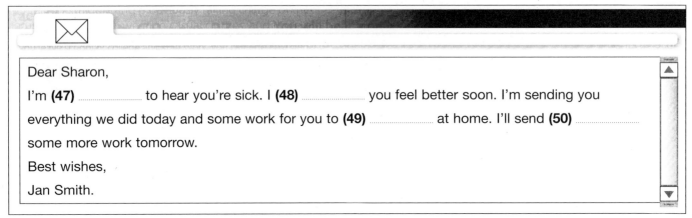

Dear Sharon,

I'm **(47)** .... to hear you're sick. I **(48)** .... you feel better soon. I'm sending you

everything we did today and some work for you to **(49)** .... at home. I'll send **(50)** ....

some more work tomorrow.

Best wishes,

Jan Smith.

Questions 51–55

Read the information about a photo competition.
Complete the application form.
For questions **51–55**, write the information on your answer sheet.

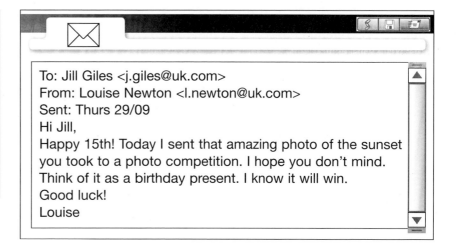

Best Photo Competition

Are you 10–16 years old?
Do you love taking photos?
Send us your best photo.
You could win £100!
Competition closes
Friday 30th September.

To: Jill Giles <j.giles@uk.com>
From: Louise Newton <l.newton@uk.com>
Sent: Thurs 29/09
Hi Jill,
Happy 15th! Today I sent that amazing photo of the sunset you took to a photo competition. I hope you don't mind. Think of it as a birthday present. I know it will win.
Good luck!
Louise

Competition application form

First name: *Jill*

Surname:	**51**
Age:	**52**
Date:	**53**
Email address:	**54**
What is your photo of?	**55**

Part 9

Question 56

Read this postcard from your English friend Matthew.

> Hi!
> This is a postcard of my town. What's your town like? What's your favourite part of your town? What do you do at weekends? Send me a postcard – I'd love to see it.
> Matt.

Write Matthew a postcard. Answer the questions.
Write **25–35** words.
Write the postcard on your answer sheet.

Part 1

Questions 1–5

You will hear five short conversations.
You will hear each conversation twice.
There is one question for each conversation.
For each question, choose the right answer (**A**, **B** or **C**).

Example:

0 What was the weather like yesterday?

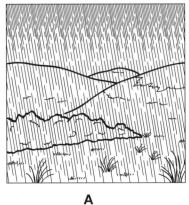  

         A   **B**   Ⓒ

1 How many people came to the picnic?

18	20	25
A	B	C

2 What did the girl cook today?

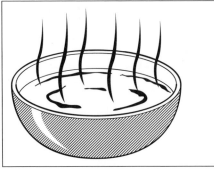  

         A   **B**   **C**

3 Which desk is the boy going to buy?

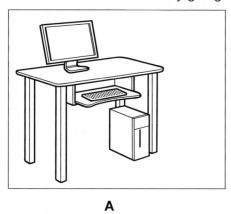

A

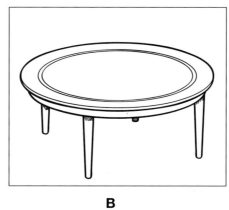

B

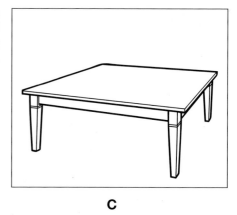

C

4 Which is the boy's family?

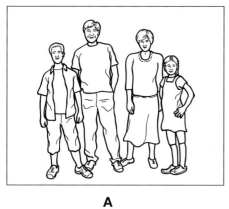

A

B

C

5 Where is the sports centre?

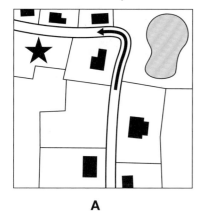

A

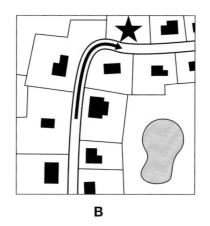

B

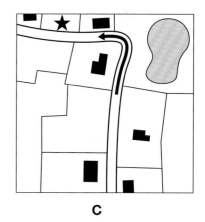

C

Part 2

Listen to Doug talking to a friend about his birthday presents.
What present did each person give him?
For questions **6–10,** write a letter **A–H** next to each person.
You will hear the conversation twice.

Example:

0   mum and dad $\boxed{\text{A}}$

	PEOPLE				**PRESENTS**	
6	sister	☐		A	bike
7	grandma	☐		B	book
8	Tony	☐		C	camera
9	Penny	☐		D	CD
10	George	☐		E	jeans
				F	skateboard
				G	T-shirt
				H	video game

Part 3

Listen to Nora talking to her friend about a film she saw.
For each question, choose the right answer (**A**, **B** or **C**).
You will hear the conversation twice.

Example:

0   What is the name of the film Nora saw?

    A   *The Vampire*

    B   *Star Game*

    (C)   *The Girl Next Door*

---

11   What is the name of the main character in the film?

    A   Georgie

    B   Matilda

    C   Patricia

12   Where is the cinema Nora went to?

    A   on George Street

    B   on Green Street

    C   in the shopping centre

13   What time does the film actually start?

    A   6.00

    B   6.30

    C   6.45

14   When will Nora's friend go to see the film?

    A   Friday

    B   Saturday

    C   Sunday

15   How much do tickets cost on Sundays?

    A   £5

    B   £7

    C   £2

You will hear a girl, Antonia, asking her friend about French lessons.
Listen and complete each question.
You will hear the conversation twice.

French classes

Place: French School

Days: **(16)** .... and Thursday

Time: **(17)** 6.00 – ....

Price: **(18)** .... per month

Phone number: **(19)** ....

Teacher: **(20)** Michelle

Part 5

You will hear some information about a new TV programme.
Listen and complete each question.
You will hear the information twice.

New TV programme

TV programme: Ask Me a Question

Channel 3 at: **(21)** .... pm

Day: **(22)** ....

Number of questions answered each week: **(23)** ....

Prize: **(24)** ....

Competition: three   **(25)** .... each week

Part 1

In class

Work in pairs. Take turns to ask and answer these questions.

1   What time do you go to school in the morning?

2   How do you get to school?

3   What sports do you like?

4   How often do you play sport?

5   What do you like to do when you're with your friends?

6   Tell me something about your favourite shop.

At home

Answer the questions on your own. You might want to record yourself so that you can play it back and hear yourself speak. What did you do well? What do you need to work on?

Part 2

Candidate A

A, here is some information about **a new computer game**. (Turn to page 141.)

B, you don't know anything about **the computer game**, so ask **A** some questions about it.

New computer game

- what/name?

- where/buy?

- how many/players?

- for children?

- cost?

Candidate B

B, here is some information about **a new film**. (Turn to page 143.)

A, you don't know anything about **the film**, so ask **B** some questions about it.

NEW FILM

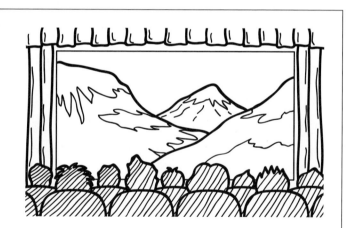

- name/film?

- where/see?

- for teenagers?

- go/Sunday?

- time?

Speaking File

Speaking Part 1 – Answering personal questions

Tips:
Extend your answers. Say more than just one word.
Ask the examiner to repeat if you have not understood.
If you can't remember the word for something, say it another way.

Talking about yourself

I'm good at …
I really like/don't like …
I enjoy/love …
I'm not good at …
I don't like/enjoy …
My favourite … is …
There are three people in my family.

Explaining

I mean …

Giving reasons

because …

Giving your opinion

I think/don't think …
I believe/don't believe …

Asking the examiner for clarification

Can you repeat that please?
Sorry, what did you say?
Did you say … ?
What is … ?

Role play

Work with a partner. Take it in turns to ask and answer questions about each other.
1   Student A: Look at the questions below.
    Student B: Look at the information on page 144.
    Student A, ask your partner these questions.
    What's your name?
    How do you spell your surname?
    How old are you?
    Where do you live?
    What is your favourite subject at school?
    Tell me something about your family.

    Student B, read your role card. When your partner asks you his/her questions, answer them using the information on the role card.

2 **Student B: Look at the questions below.**
Student A: Look at the information on page 139.
Student B, ask your partner these questions.
What's your name?
How do you spell your surname?
How old are you?
Where do you live?
Which subject do you find the hardest at school?
Tell me something about your school.

Student A, read your role card. When your partner asks you his/her questions, answer them using the information on the role card.

Speaking Part 2 – Asking and answering questions

Tips:
When asking questions, think of the type of information you need and then choose the appropriate question word.
When answering questions, ask your partner for clarification if you have not understood.

Asking for information

Price
How much is the student ticket?
How much does it cost?

Address
Where is it?
What is the address?

Name
What is the name of the school/shop/etc.?

Email/phone
What is the email address?
What is the phone number?

Dates/days/times
When is/are the … ?
Is it open/closed on Mondays, etc.?
What time does it open/close?
What time is it on?

Other information
What can you do/learn there?
What can you win?
Is it for children/teenagers?
Does it sell … ?
Can you buy … ?
What can you see there?
Is there a car park?

Answering questions

Yes/no questions
Positive answers
Yes, it is.
Yes, you can.
Yes, it's …
Yes, it's open on Mondays, etc.
Yes, the phone number is …
Yes, the email address is …
Negative answers
No, it isn't.
No, you can't.
No, it's closed on Mondays, etc.

Wh- questions
The name of … is …
The address is …
It's in … Street.
It's on … Road.
The phone number is …
The email address is …

Asking your partner for clarification

Can you repeat (your question), please?
Sorry, what did you say?
I don't understand what you mean.
Do you mean … ?

Asking for and giving information

1 **Student A**
   Ask for information about a film. Use these prompts to help you form
   your questions.
1 name/film?
2 actors?
3 where/show?
4 time/Sunday?
5 price/student ticket?

Student B

Use the information on page 144 to answer your partner's questions.

2 **Student B**
   Ask for information about an exhibition. Use these prompts to help you form your
   questions.
1 name/exhibition?
2 what/see?
3 open/every day?
4 opening times/Sunday?
5 more information?

Student A

Use the information on page 139 to answer your partner's questions.

Writing File

Writing Part 9 – an email or a postcard

If you are writing an email or a postcard, follow these tips.
Imagine you are writing to someone you know well. Think of interesting ways to answer his/her questions.
Use short forms, e.g 'I've just painted' not 'I have just painted'.
Greet them and say goodbye in a friendly way.

Sample question

Read the email from your English friend, Matt.

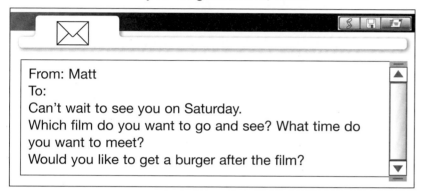

From: Matt
To:
Can't wait to see you on Saturday.
Which film do you want to go and see? What time do you want to meet?
Would you like to get a burger after the film?

Write an email to Matt and answer the questions.
Write **25–35** words.
Write the email on your answer sheet.

Sample answer

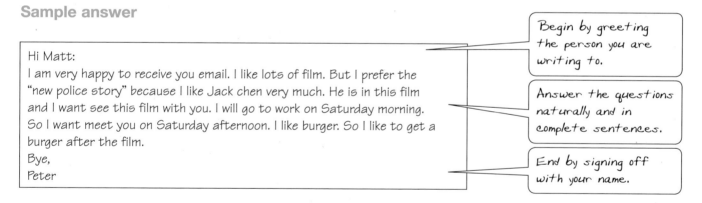

Hi Matt:
I am very happy to receive you email. I like lots of film. But I prefer the "new police story" because I like Jack chen very much. He is in this film and I want see this film with you. I will go to work on Saturday morning. So I want meet you on Saturday afternoon. I like burger. So I like to get a burger after the film.
Bye,
Peter

Begin by greeting the person you are writing to.

Answer the questions naturally and in complete sentences.

End by signing off with your name.

Examiner's comments

All three parts of the message are clearly communicated. There are no spelling errors but there are occasional grammar errors and punctuation errors. It's quite long (69 words) but this is not penalised. **5 marks**
Check you have:
- begun with a greeting and ended by signing off with your name.
- answered all three questions in the prompt.
- communicated your message as clearly as possible.
- written between 25 and 35 words.
- written in an informal style.

Writing Part 9 – a notice

If you are writing a notice, follow these tips.
Give your notice a heading and underline it, e.g. Lost.
Be clear about what you want to communicate.
End the notice with your name.

Sample question

You have lost your new mobile phone. Write a notice to put on the wall at your school.

Say:

- **where** you lost your mobile phone.

- **what** your mobile phone looks like.

- **how** to return it to you.

Sample answer

Begin with a heading.

Include all the information in the bullet points.

End by writing your name.

> **Lost**
>
> I lost my new mobile phone in the cafeteria yesterday. It's a small black Samsung phone with a large screen. Please give it to Ms Smith in Room 10 if you find it.
>
> Thanks,
>
> Rachel

Examiner's comments

All three parts of the message are clearly communicated. There are no spelling or grammar errors. **5 marks**
Check you have:

- given your notice a heading.
- written your name at the end.
- included all three pieces of information in the prompt.
- communicated your message as clearly as possible.
- written between 25 and 35 words.

Writing Part 9 – a note

If you are writing a note, follow these tips.
Imagine you are writing to someone you know well or to a member of your family. Give some specific details about the things, people or places you talk about.
Use short forms, e.g. 'I'm going to the cinema' not 'I am going to the cinema'.
Greet them and say goodbye in a friendly way.

Sample question

You are going out. Leave a note for your parents. Tell them:

- **where** you are going.

- **who** you are going with

- **what** time you will be home.

Sample answer

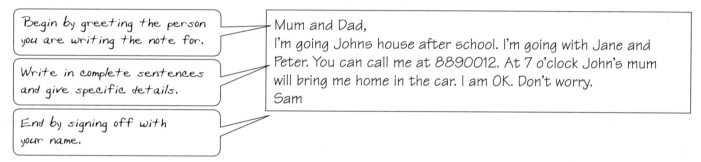

Begin by greeting the person you are writing the note for.

Write in complete sentences and give specific details.

End by signing off with your name.

Mum and Dad,
I'm going Johns house after school. I'm going with Jane and Peter. You can call me at 8890012. At 7 o'clock John's mum will bring me home in the car. I am OK. Don't worry.
Sam

Examiner's comments

All three parts of the message are clearly communicated. There are no spelling errors but there are occasional grammar errors. **5 marks**

Check your writing
Check you have:
- begun with a greeting and ended by signing off with your name.
- included all three pieces of information in the prompt.
- communicated your message as clearly as possible.
- written between 25 and 35 words.
- written in an informal style.

KET for Schools Top 20 Questions

1 **What is the format of the KET for Schools exam, and are all the papers taken on the same day?**
There are three papers:
Reading and Writing (1 hour 10 minutes)
Listening (about 30 minutes)
Speaking (8–10 minutes)
Papers 1 and 2 are always taken on the same day. The Speaking test may be taken on the same day or on a different day.

2 **How is KET for Schools different from KET?**
KET for Schools follows the same format as KET. The difference is that the content and topics in KET for Schools are more suitable for the interests and experiences of younger people.

3 **What level is KET for Schools?**
KET is aligned to the Council of Europe Common European Framework for Reference (CEFR). KET is level A2 in the CEFR.

4 **Is KET for Schools suitable for teenagers from any culture?**
Yes. All tasks are written to avoid any cultural bias.

5 **What are the grade ranges for KET for Schools?**
There are four grades with fixed values:
Pass with merit = 85–100%
Pass = 70–84%
A1 = 45–69%
Fail = 44% and below

6 **Do I have to pass each paper in order to pass the exam?**
No. Each paper doesn't have a pass or fail mark. The final mark a candidate gets in KET for Schools is an average mark obtained by adding the marks for all three papers together.

7 **What mark do I need to get to pass the exam overall?**
To achieve a pass in the KET for Schools exam a candidate must receive a minimum of 70% as an overall average.

8 **When can I use pens or pencils in the exam?**
In KET for Schools a candidate must use pencil in all papers.

9 **If I write entirely in capital letters, does this affect my score?**
No. Candidates are not penalised for writing in capitals in the exam.

10 **Am I allowed to use a dictionary?**
No.

11 **Is correct spelling important in Paper 1 (Reading and Writing)?**
It is important only in Parts 6, 7 and 8.

12 **Is correct spelling important in Paper 2 (Listening)?**
It is important only in Parts 4 and 5.

13 **In Paper 1 (Reading and Writing) will extra time be given for me to transfer my answers to the answer sheet?**
No. You must transfer them in the 1 hour and 10 minutes you are given to complete the exam in.

14 **In Paper 2 (Listening) will extra time be given for me to transfer my answers to the answer sheet?**
Yes. You will be given some time at the end of the test for this.

15 **How many times will I hear each recording in Paper 2 (Listening)?**
You will hear each recording twice.

16 **Can I ask any questions if I don't understand something in Papers 1 (Reading and Writing) and 2 (Listening)?**
The only questions you can ask are those that relate to the rules of the exam. For example, the time you have, where to write your name or your answers, completing the answer sheet, whether or not you can use a pen, etc. You cannot ask for any help with the test items themselves.

17 **Can I ask any questions if I don't understand something in Paper 3 (Speaking)?**
Yes. You can ask the examiner to repeat a question in Part 1 and to repeat the instructions in Part 2. If you still don't understand, tell the examiner you don't understand. You can ask your partner to repeat or clarify when they are asking you questions or answering your questions in Part 2.

18 **In Paper 3 (Speaking), do I have to go in with another student? Can I choose my partner?**
You cannot be examined alone. You will usually be examined with one other candidate, but if you are one of the last candidates to be examined and there is an odd number of candidates on the day, you may be examined in a group of three. In some smaller centres you may be able to choose your partner, but in bigger centres this may not be possible.

19 **In Paper 3 (Speaking), is it a good idea for me to prepare what I am going to say in Part 1?**
It's a good idea to practise saying your name, spelling your surname and talking about yourself (your family, school, school subjects, hobbies, etc.). It is important that you answer the examiner's questions and that you do so naturally, so listen carefully and think about the questions you have been asked. If you give a prepared speech you may not answer the examiner's question. You will lose marks if your answers are irrelevant.

20 **In Paper 3 (Speaking), what if I can't understand my partner in Part 2 or if he/she can't understand me?**
If there is a communication breakdown between you and your partner in Part 2, try to solve the problem between you. For example, ask your partner for clarification or to repeat a question or an answer, or help your partner if necessary. You will be given credit for helping your partner if he/she is having difficulty.

Answer sheets

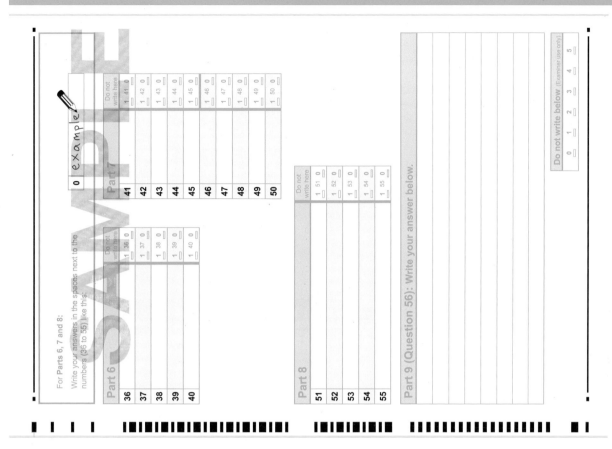

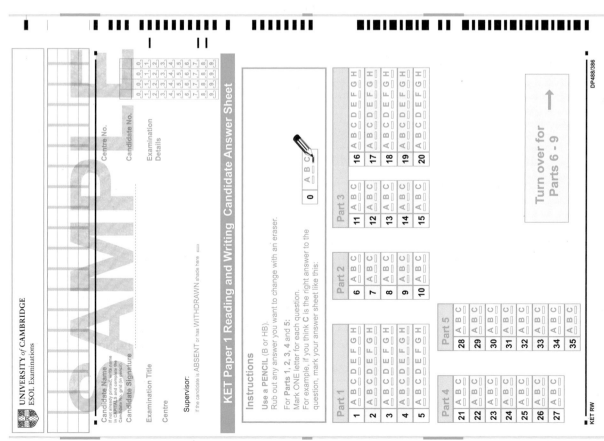

For Parts 6, 7 and 8:

Write your answers in the spaces next to the numbers (36 to 55) like this:

	0	example

Part 6

		Do not write here
36		1 36 0
37		1 37 0
38		1 38 0
39		1 39 0
40		1 40 0

Part 7

		Do not write here
41		1 41 0
42		1 42 0
43		1 43 0
44		1 44 0
45		1 45 0
46		1 46 0
47		1 47 0
48		1 48 0
49		1 49 0
50		1 50 0

Part 8

		Do not write here
51		1 51 0
52		1 52 0
53		1 53 0
54		1 54 0
55		1 55 0

Part 9 (Question 56): Write your answer below.

Do not write below (Examiner use only)

0 1 2 3 4 5

UNIVERSITY of CAMBRIDGE
ESOL Examinations

Candidate Name
If not already printed, write name in CAPITALS and complete the Candidate No. grid (in pencil)

Candidate Signature

Examination Title

Centre

Supervisor:
If the candidate is ABSENT or has WITHDRAWN shade here

Centre No.

Candidate No.

Examination Details

KET Paper 1 Reading and Writing Candidate Answer Sheet

Instructions

Use a **PENCIL** (B or HB).
Rub out any answer you want to change with an eraser.

For **Parts 1, 2, 3, 4** and **5**:
Mark **ONE** letter for each question.
For example, if you think **C** is the right answer to the question, mark your answer sheet like this:

0	A B C

Part 1

1	A B C D E F G H
2	A B C D E F G H
3	A B C D E F G H
4	A B C D E F G H
5	A B C D E F G H

Part 2

6	A B C
7	A B C
8	A B C
9	A B C
10	A B C

Part 3

11	A B C
12	A B C
13	A B C
14	A B C
15	A B C
16	A B C D E F G H
17	A B C D E F G H
18	A B C D E F G H
19	A B C D E F G H
20	A B C D E F G H

Part 4

21	A B C
22	A B C
23	A B C
24	A B C
25	A B C
26	A B C
27	A B C

Part 5

28	A B C
29	A B C
30	A B C
31	A B C
32	A B C
33	A B C
34	A B C
35	A B C

Turn over for
Parts 6 - 9

KET RW

DP488/386

UNIVERSITY *of* **CAMBRIDGE**
ESOL Examinations

SAMPLE

Candidate Name
If not already printed, write name
in CAPITALS and complete the
Candidate No. grid (in pencil).

Candidate Signature

Examination Title

Centre

Supervisor:
If the candidate is ABSENT or has WITHDRAWN shade here ▭

Centre No.

Candidate No.

Examination Details

0	0	0	0
1	1	1	1
2	2	2	2
3	3	3	3
4	4	4	4
5	5	5	5
6	6	6	6
7	7	7	7
8	8	8	8
9	9	9	9

KET Paper 2 Listening Candidate Answer Sheet

Instructions

Use a PENCIL (B or HB).

Rub out any answer you want to change with an eraser.

For **Parts 1, 2** and **3**:
Mark ONE letter for each question.
For example, if you think **C** is the right answer to the
question, mark your answer sheet like this:

0	A B C

Part 1		**Part 2**		**Part 3**	
1	A B C	6	A B C D E F G H	11	A B C
2	A B C	7	A B C D E F G H	12	A B C
3	A B C	8	A B C D E F G H	13	A B C
4	A B C	9	A B C D E F G H	14	A B C
5	A B C	10	A B C D E F G H	15	A B C

For **Parts 4** and **5**:
Write your answers in the spaces next to the
numbers (16 to 25) like this:

0	example

Part 4		Do not write here
16		1 16 0
17		1 17 0
18		1 18 0
19		1 19 0
20		1 20 0

Part 5		Do not write here
21		1 21 0
22		1 22 0
23		1 23 0
24		1 24 0
25		1 25 0

KET L

DP314/088

Part 1 Activity, Role play, Student A (page 130)

Student A – role card
Your name is Paulo Cometti. You are 13 years old and you live in Palermo, Italy. You like school and but you find maths very difficult. Your school is very large. It is new and your class has a great view of the sea. You like most of your teachers and you have a lot of good friends at school. You walk to school on foot every morning.

Part 2 Activity, Asking for and giving information, Student A (page 132)

The Titanic Exhibition

Now on at Highgate Museum
Come and see more than 200 objects found on the ship.
Don't wait too long. The exhibition ends on 28th February.
Museum opening times:
Mondays closed
Tuesday – Friday: 10.00 am – 6.00 pm
Weekends: 10.00 am – 8.00 pm
Price: €5 adults, €2.50 students.
For more information visit our website www.highgatemuseum.com

Test 1, Part 2, Candidate A (page 39)

Junior Athletics Club

56 James Street
Are you 10–16 years old? Come
and join our athletics club.
Training: Mondays and
Wednesdays 4–6 p.m.
Visit: www.athletics.com

Test 2, Part 2, Candidate A (page 57)

Max's Birthday Party

You are invited to
Max's birthday party
Sunday 5th June at 1 p.m.
63 Green Street
Let me know if you
can come.
Call me on 456 7890.

Test 3, Part 2, Candidate A (page 75)

Art Museum

Modern art exhibition now on.
More than 50 works of art to see.
Open Tuesday – Sunday 10am – 5pm
ROOF TOP CAFÉ
FREE PARKING
Tickets:
Adults £7.00 Students and children free
45 Hills Road

Lou's Animal Care Hospital

99 Beech Road

We help all animals

7 days a week

8am – 6pm

For appointments call 779065

Free parking available

PHOTOGRAPHY CLASSES

At Smith Street Primary School

Every Monday 4–5pm

Call: 4560099

Young people 10–17 welcome

The classes are free

Bring your own camera

Best Computers

29 Lang Street

New computer game:

Dinosaur

For all ages

For one to two players

£20

Alan's Music School

Smith Street Shopping Centre
We'll teach you to play guitar, piano or the drums.
Classes 3 to 5 p.m. Every Saturday
Fee: £5 per lesson
Phone: 265 0828

Pete's Books
117 Jones Street
Get your schoolbooks here.
Open seven days of the week
9am – 5pm.
Telephone: 267 8911

Bike Race
for anyone 11–16 years old at
OLYMPIC STADIUM
3rd August
Prizes

First prize: New bike
Second prize: MP3 player
Third prize: £50

Visit http://www.bikerace.com/ for more information

Tennis Lessons

Will's Tennis School
Country Road
€20 per hour
Classes every afternoon
Call 2987655 to make an appointment.
Bring your own tennis racket.

Fred's DVD Club

67 Green Street
Rent films and games for all ages
Open 10am–10pm
every day
Phone: 3455678
www.Freds.com

NOW SHOWING AT THE
VILLAGE CINEMA

THE FARM

A NEW FILM FOR ALL AGES
SESSIONS: 5.30 PM AND 7.30 PM
EVERY DAY
HTTP://WWW.VILLAGE.COM/

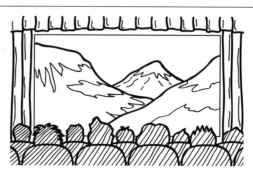

Visuals for Speaking File B

Part 1 Activity, Role play, Student B (page 131)

Student B – role card
Your name is Patricia Anderson. You are 14 years old and you live in Stockholm, Sweden. You love school and you especially like learning English. You have a mother and father, three sisters and two brothers. You are the youngest in your family. Your family all live together and they enjoy doing lots of outdoor activities together.

Part 2 Activity, Asking for and giving information, Student B (page 132)

THE GREAT RACE
starring Peter Little and Olivia Holland.

NOW SHOWING AT THE REGENT CINEMA.
SESSIONS START AT 6.00 PM EVERY AFTERNOON.
PRICE: £10 ADULTS, £7 STUDENTS.
YOU CAN BOOK TICKETS BY CALLING 8898 0978.

Answer key

TEST 1 Paper 1 Reading and Writing

Part 1 Guidance

Exercise 1
1 5   2 8   3 on your answer sheet

Exercise 2
1 *in the classroom*   2 *food or drinks*

Exercise 3
<u>No talking</u> during test = You must be quiet when this is happening.
<u>Found</u> — a small black purse – see Ms Smith = See this person if you have lost something.
<u>Quiet please</u> = You should not talk in this place.

Exercise 4
can = able to
cannot = not able to
must = need to
must not = do not
should not = it's not a good idea to
should = it's a good idea to

Exercise 5
1 cannot   2 should not   3 must   4 must   5 should not

Part 1

1 B   2 F   3 E   4 G   5 D

Part 2 Guidance

Exercise 1
1 eating   2 to be   3 doing   4 playing OR to play   5 to do

Exercise 2
1 A comes   B goes   C takes
2 A play   B do   C makes
3 A watch   B saw   C looked
4 A already   B yet   C ever
5 A plan   B think   C decided

Part 2

6 C (You *play* a video game not *make* or *do* a video game.)
7 C (You *make a friend. Make* collocates with *friend*.)
8 C (You *go to school*. You *take the bus to school*. If you are at school when you are saying this, then you can say they *come to school*. In this case this is wrong.)
9 A (We say *at the weekend* but *in the afternoon* and *in the day*.)
10 A (*Free time* means leisure time. The others have the wrong meaning for this sentence.)

Part 3 Guidance

Exercise 1
Yes, it is.

Exercise 2
1 A a friend to another friend, a family member to another family member or friend
   B two strangers have just met   C a teacher to a student
   D a friend to another friend   E a friend to another friend

Exercise 3
1 B   2 D   3 E   4 A   5 C

Exercise 4
1 Yolanda and Maria.
2 On the phone.

Exercise 5
1 To see what Yolanda is doing on Saturday.
2 No, she can't because she's going shopping with her mum.
3 On Sunday.

Part 3

11 A	12 C	13 A	14 C	15 B
16 A	17 H	18 B	19 E	20 F

Part 4 Guidance

Exercise 1
1 7
2 Decide if the sentences are right or wrong, or if the text doesn't say.
3 Jessica Watson.
4 On your answer sheet.

Exercise 4
Because Jessica did sail around the world when she was only 16.
'16-year-old Jessica Watson set out to do something no one her age had ever done before – to sail around the world ... She started her trip in Sydney ... ended up back in Sydney ... .'

Exercise 5
21 Jessica <u>started</u> and <u>ended</u> her trip <u>from the same city</u>.
22 Jessica took a little <u>more than 7 months</u> to complete the journey.
23 Jessica returned to Sydney <u>on the day of her birthday</u>.
24 Mike Perham <u>was two years older that Jessica when he sailed around the world</u>.
25 When Jessica arrived back in Sydney, <u>there were many people there to greet her</u>.
26 Jessica sailed <u>2000 nautical miles more than anyone else</u>.
27 Jessica said she will <u>sail around the world again next year</u>.

Part 4

21 A (She started her trip in Sydney, Australia, on her 10-metre boat ... she finally ended up back in Sydney Harbour on 15th May 2010)
22 B (...and after 7 long months alone at sea she finally ended up back in Sydney ...)
23 C
24 B (16-year-old Jessica Watson .... Perham had sailed around the world the previous year at the age of 17)
25 A (...she got a hero's welcome with thousands of people there to greet her ...)
26 B (...she needed to have sailed 2000 nautical miles more than she did to break the world record ...)
27 C

Part 5 Guidance

Exercise 1
1 a child actor   2 8

Exercise 2
Because the expression is 'at the age of ... '.

Exercise 3

1 at	2 on AND by	3 on	4 to	5 in
6 to	7 in	8 of	9 at	

Exercise 4

1 yours	2 There	3 everyone	4 many	5 Many
6 some				

Exercise 5

1 seen	2 staying	3 went	4 reading	5 go

Exercise 6

1 but	2 so	3 because	4 and

Part 5

28 B (*has + continued*, which is past participle of *continue*; *will + continue*; *is + continuing*)
29 C (*Like* is used to give examples that are noun phrases – *like + War of the Worlds*)
30 C (*Many* is used for countable nouns in their plural form – e.g. *people*. *Every* needs the singular noun *person*; *Few people* means not many, which is wrong here.)
31 B (*the* continues the pattern in the sentence – *the big screen and the lights*. We are also talking about the big screen in general.)
32 A (You *learn to do* something. *Learn* is followed by the full infinitive.)
33 B (Love is followed by the patterns verb-*ing* or the full infinitive. So *love watching* or *love to watch* would be correct here.)
34 C (*Can* means she is able to play the violin. *Must* and *should* are both wrong here.)
35 A (The subject of the statement is *she*, so this is what needs to go in the tag question.)

Part 6 Guidance

Exercise 1
moon – noun
mountain – noun
yesterday – adverb
winter – noun
swim – verb
catch – verb
cheap – adjective
closed – adjective

Part 6

36 neighbour	37 friend	38 cousin	39 married	40 guest

Part 7 Guidance

Exercise 1

1	adjective	2	adjective	3	verb	4	noun

Exercise 2

1	favourite	2	last	3	goes	4	film

Exercise 3

1	to	2	on	3	him	4	it OR them	5	where
6	or	7	the	8	a				

Part 7

41 you (a subject pronoun is needed here)
42 ask (a verb is needed here)
43 what (= the thing which)
44 good/great (a positive adjective is needed here)
45 see (a verb is needed here)
46 doing (verb+*ing* is needed here because the verb is in the present continuous)
47 me/out (either an object – *help me* – or an adverb as part of the phrasal verb *help out*)
48 the (the definite article is needed here)
49 take/drive (a verb that collocates with *home* is needed here)
50 know (the expression *Let me know* is needed here)

Part 8 Guidance

Exercise 1
1 an invitation and a text message
2 some notes
Exercise 2
52 The time is wrong.
53 He/she hasn't included a drink.
54 The spelling of 'comfortable' is wrong.
55 The activity is wrong.
The correct answers should be:
52 11.00 am
53 a sandwich and some orange juice
54 comfortable walking shoes
55 a long walk
Exercise 3
1 Gina and Paul
2 Gina
3 Sunday 14th May
4 1 p.m.
5 Paul
6 (Paul's) mum can drive
7 12.30

Part 8

51 Sunday 14th May	52 1 p.m.	53 Paul	54 car	55 12.30

Part 9 Guidance

Exercise 1
1 Matt
2 an email
3 Which film do you want to go and see? What time do you want to meet? Would you like to get a burger after the film?

Exercise 2
1 Ruth has answered all three questions correctly. Monica hasn't.
2 Ruth has. Monica hasn't written enough.
3 Ruth's is better because she has followed the instructions.

Part 9

Hi Matt,
Thanks for your email. We can go to see Toy Story 3. I've heard it's very good. Let's meet at 5.00. I'd love to get a burger after the film.
See you soon.
Bye,
John
This answer is good because:
• it answers the three questions in the email from Matt.
• it clearly communicates the writer's message.
• it is between 25–35 words long (it is 33 words long).
• it is an informal email.

Test 1 Paper 2 Listening

Part 1 Guidance

Exercise 1
You should underline 'six', 'quarter past six', 'half past six', 'seven' and 'quarter to seven'.

Exercise 2
C is correct because that is the time that they agree to meet.

Exercise 5
1 b	2 b	3 b	4 a
5 a	6 a		

Exercise 7
1 star	2 triangle	3 square	4 rectangle OR oblong
5 circle			

Exercise 8
A has circles on the cover, B has a plain cover and C has stars on the cover.

Exercise 9
4	A tennis	B football	C basketball
5	A soup	B spaghetti	C chicken

Part 1

1 C (What? So you got them for £30? ... Yep! Sure did.)
2 A (Mine's green with lots of yellow circles on the cover.)
3 A (Actually, no we counted them and there are 25.)
4 A (What about tennis? I was thinking of doing that Saturday mornings?)
5 C (You'll just have to have the chicken I'm afraid.)

Part 2 Guidance

Exercise 3
1 2
2 Pete. We don't know his friend's name.
3 They are friends.
4 holiday plans
5 Pete

Exercise 4
You should underline 'brother', 'sister' and 'mum'.

Exercise 5
Brother = T-shirt
Sister = CD
Mum = flowers

Exercise 6
book, purse

Part 2

6 A (...on Tuesday I might go to the cinema with Josh.)
7 G (On Wednesday, I'm going swimming with Paul and Toby.)
8 E (Thursday ...um... I haven't planned anything for Thursday.)
9 F (But on Friday I'm going shopping for some new clothes.)
10 C (I'm playing a match next Saturday.)

Part 3 Guidance

Exercise 1
1 The speakers are Darren and his friend, Maria.
2 They will be talking about a book report they have to write.
3 They will mention the name of the book, how much Darren has read, when Darren returned to school, when Darren read the book and when he will call Maria.

Exercise 2
11 How much of the book has Darren read?
12 The name of the book is
13 Darren returned to school on
14 When did Darren read the book?
15 On Sunday, Darren will call Maria at

Exercise 3
1

Exercise 4
A

Part 3

11 B (I haven't actually read the book yet.)
12 A (*Flight 221*)
13 A (I was away from school from 2nd November until the 20th.)
14 B (I'll read it over the weekend ...)
15 C (I'll be out then. Call me at 7. ... OK.)

Parts 4 and 5 Guidance

Exercise 1
| 16 = A | 17 = D | 18 = B | 19 = C | 20 = E |

Exercise 3
| 1 8456-7890 | 2 66-77-8901 | 3 049-876-1233 | 4 039-789-9961 |

Exercise 5
| 1 £4.99 | 2 60p | 3 £70 | 4 £14.40 |

Exercise 7
| 1 Lester | 2 Macintosh | 3 Ian | 4 Sean | 5 Lisbeth |

Part 4

16 £80 (Let's see. £100 with 20% off comes to £80.)
17 Friday (Can you hold it for me till Friday? ... I can do that. You'll need to come in by 5.00 o'clock though.)
18 5/5.00 (You'll need to come in by 5 o'clock though.)
19 Lowe (Lowe. That's L.O.W.E.)
20 345 3799 (It's 345 3799.)

Part 5

21 Friday (... the school concert is on this Friday night.)
22 7/7.00 (The concert starts at 7.30 but be please be here half an hour before that ...)
23 Tuesday (... band practice on Tuesday and Thursday afternoon at 4pm.)
24 3B (The practice will be held in room 3B.)
25 231 2117 (If you can't come, let us know. Call the office on 231 2117 and leave a message.)

Test 1 Paper 3 Speaking

Part 1 Guidance

Exercise 2
| 1 Sweeney | 2 Armstrong | 3 Charlene | 4 Moneypenny |

Exercise 4
| 1 h | 2 c | 3 b OR g | 4 b OR g | 5 f |
| 6 e | 7 d | 8 a | | |

Part 2 Guidance

Exercise 1
1   Where are the lessons?
2   What time are the lessons?
3   How much do the lessons cost?
4   What's the address?
5   Can you tell me the telephone number?

Exercise 2
You can say 1, 4, 5 and 6.
You shouldn't say 2 and 3 because they can sound rude.

Part 2

Possible questions:
Athletics club
What is the name of the club?
Is it for children?
Does it have a website?
When is the training?
What is the address?

Alan's music school
Where is the school?
What can you learn (there)?
How much does it cost?
When are the classes?
What is the phone number?

Test 2 Paper 1 Reading and Writing

Part 1

1 C	2 D	3 F	4 H	5 B

Part 2

6   B   (The possessive adjective *your* means *favourite* is the correct answer.)
7   B   (At a café you *buy* something, which means you pay for it. If you *take* it, you steal it. *Do* is wrong.)
8   A   (*Member* collocates with *club*.)
9   B   (*Kinds* means *types*. The other options are wrong.)
10 C   (*Says* is followed by *that* + subject + verb. *Tells* takes an object – you tell someone something. *Thinks* means it is his opinion, which is the wrong meaning here.)

Part 3

11 B	12 C	13 A	14 A	15 A
16 B	17 H	18 G	19 F	20 C

Part 4

21 C   (Each week, Tony Moldino, an artist himself, shows you how to make an amazing work of art.)
22 B   (Each week, Tony Moldino, ...)
23 C   (*Dance School* is a new teen drama about a group of students who all want to become dancers.)
24 C   (The story is told through the eyes of Tina Giles, a farm girl who ...)
25 B   (On her first day at the school she meets Joe, Heather and John.)
26 B   (It follows the funny times of Bert and his family in a small town in America.)
27 B   (Bert isn't happy because he too wants to be in the play.)

Part 5

28 C   (*Most* is used for countable nouns in their plural form – e.g. *people*. *Every* and *Each* need the singular noun *person*.)
29 B   (*Like* collocates with *look* to refer to appearance.)
30 A   (*But* introduces a contrast here.)
31 C   (The infinitive verb *eat* means that a modal verb is needed here. *Will* means that is what it does – it eats other animals. *Must* is wrong because the devil is not obliged to eat other animals, it just does because it is a carnivore.)
32 A   (*It* is followed by the verb in the third person, which takes an *s*. *Doing* needs the verb *be*.)
33 C   (*Yet* is used with questions and negative statements. *Since* is followed by a point of time in the past.)

34 B (The pattern that follows *means* is *means + that*. *Which* and *when* are relative pronouns. They need to be used with relative clauses.)

35 C (*Can* expresses possibility here. It is possible that the mother devil looks after four babies at a time.)

Part 6

36 subject   37 uniform   38 teacher   39 homework   40 dictionary

Part 7

41 to (*tried* + the infinitive with *to*)
42 near (a preposition of place is needed here)
43 like (The expression is *I would like*)
44 I (a subject pronoun is needed here)
45 the (the definite article is needed here)
46 at (a preposition is needed here)
47 There (*There is* means it exists)
48 road (*the road* collocates with *across*)
49 it (an object pronoun is needed here)
50 because (*because* introduces a reason here)

Part 8

51 David MacDonald
52 No acting experience/none
53 Romeo
54 9876541
55 d.macdonald@horizon.com

Part 9

Hi Mum and Dad
I'm going to the cinema with Kate and Tom. We're going to se a film at Bay Cinema on Smith Street. I'll be home around 7.00. I'll call you later.
Bye,
Maria.
This answer is good because:
• it deals with all three points.
• it clearly communicates the writer's message.
• it is between 25 and 35 words long (it is 30 words long).
• it is an informal note.

Test 2 Paper 2 Listening

Part 1

1 A (I didn't hear anything about rain. Just cold and windy, so you can wear your new shoes.)
2 B (I told him to meet us outside the newsagent's on the corner.)
3 B (Oh that is beautiful. The trees are lovely.)
4 A (On second thoughts just make it three chocolate cones.)
5 B (He said he'd be here by 8.30.)

Part 2

6   B (My sister's hobby is cycling. She's just bought herself a new bike.)
7   G (He's a swimmer.)
8   H (… she plays tennis every Saturday.)
9   C (No, even worse. Fishing!)
10 E (He plays golf actually.)

Part 3

11 C (From Frank's Computers.)
12 A (Frank's is on Elizabeth Street – just off Mersey Road.)
13 A (It's £500.)
14 C (My mum's going to pick it up on Friday night.)
15 B (Come over at 11.00 and bring your new game.)

16 Wednesday(s) (At the moment we only offer piano lessons on Wednesdays ...)
17 4/4–6 (Piano lessons are on between 4 and 6.)
18 £20 (It's £20.)
19 24 Banksia Street (24 Banksia Street.)
20 0985570012 (It's 0985570012.)

Part 5

21 Friday (There are performances on Fridays and Sundays only ...)
22 6/6.00/6 o'clock/6pm (The starting time for each performance is 6 pm.)
23 5.30 (To be seated in time, you will need to get to the theatre half an hour before the performance is scheduled to start.)
24 £5.50 (... and £5.50 for children.)
25 3459088 (That's 3459088.)

Test 2 Paper 3 Speaking

Part 2

Possible questions:

<u>Birthday party</u>
What is the name of the boy?/What is the boy's name?
When is the party?
What time is the party?
What is the phone number?
What is the address?

<u>Bookshop</u>
What is the name of the bookshop?
Is it open on Sunday? Does it open on Sunday?
What time is it open?
Does it sell schoolbooks?
What is the phone number?

Test 3 Paper 1 Reading and Writing

Part 1

1 A	2 H	3 C	4 D	5 G

Part 2

6 A (*told* takes an object – you tell someone something. *Said* and *decided* don't.)
7 B (You *leave* your home to go to school.)
8 A (*the whole day; most of the day; all of the day*.)
9 C (If you *buy postcards*, you pay for them. If you *take them*, you steal them. You cannot *have postcards* from a shop.)
10 B (You *send* something to someone.)

Part 3

11 B	12 C	13 A	14 A	15 C
16 F	17 C	8 B	19 G	20 H

Part 4

21 B (We couldn't believe our luck when my sister and I found out that we would be spending five whole days visiting our dream theme park!)
22 C
23 A (My favourite was the one called Big Thunder Mountain.)
24 B (For example, Snow White and the Seven Dwarfs was a little boring.)
25 A (... where a guide gave us a tour.)
26 A (It was really interesting and we learnt a lot about how films and cartoons are made.)
27 C

Part 5

28 B (An auxiliary verb is needed here. We say *had not entered*. We cannot say *did not entered*. The correct form is *did not enter*. *Were* is wrong in this case.)
29 B (The correct preposition is *by*.)
30 C (*More than* is the comparative form which is needed here.)
31 A (*Watched* continues the pattern of the other verbs in the list – *read* and *played*.)
32 B (*Other* is used with plural forms, *another* with singular forms. *Their young people* is wrong.)
33 A (This is a conditional sentence so the conditional link *If* is needed.)
34 B (The infinitive *be* is needed after *would*.)
35 C (*What* is needed here. *Where* is used to refer to place and *when* to time.)

Part 6

36 campsite   37 magazine   38 join   39 photograph   40 hobby

Part 7

41 old (The expression is *14 years old*.)
42 In (A preposition is needed here.)
43 out (The adverb *out* is needed to form this phrasal verb.)
44 my (A possessive adjective is needed here.)
45 and (A link is needed here.)
46 a (The expression is *three times a week*.)
47 been (The past participle of *be* is *been*.)
48 went (The simple past form of *go* is needed here.)
49 also (A link with the previous sentence is needed here.)
50 her (A possessive adjective is needed here.)

Part 8

51 TPinto@hotpost.com (Tim Pinto's email address is needed here.)
52 *The Castle* (Today I'm going to order *The Castle* …)
53 14th May / 14/5 (Today I'm going to order …)
54 two/2 (I'll get one for you and one for me.)
55 £50 (*The Castle* – £25)

Part 9

Sample answer:
Hi Terry,
My new house is in the town centre. I really love my bedroom. It's big and I've just painted the walls blue. You can come to visit me this weekend if you like.
Bye,
John

This answer is good because:
• it answers the three questions in the email from Terry.
• it clearly communicates the writer's message.
• it is between 25 and 35 words long (it is 33 words long).
• it is an informal email.

Test 3 Paper 2 Listening

Part 1

1 A (I think I'll take the jumper …)
2 A (No, it's about 42 kilometres.)
3 A (I'll leave at around 7.00.)
4 A (Morocco? That sounds like fun.)
5 A (That's my cat, Fluffy, on my lap there … I don't have a picture of him with me. I'll bring one tomorrow to show you. I've got a nice one of him and Fluffy together.)

Part 2

6 H (Penny's watching cartoons on TV)
7 B (Oh, actually, Helen's out of the bath. She's getting dressed.)
8 F (Paul's reading a book …)
9 C (… Tim's playing on the computer.)
10 G (… he's gone to John's house.)

Part 3

11 A (I sold the last one early this afternoon.)
12 B (If you come in after school, I'll have it for you then.)
13 C (It's £6.50.)
14 A (Yes, of course. That's not a problem. I'll see you tomorrow afternoon then.)
15 B (My mum would like a copy of *The Best Cook* magazine.)

Part 4

16 Saturday (That's on Saturday the 9th May.)
17 7/7.00/7 o'clock (Actually, no. The main band comes on at 8 but the concert starts at 7 o'clock. There is another band playing at 7.)

18 3/three (Yes, three, please.)
19 Sims (Yes, it's Pat Sims.)
20 £15 (They're £15 each.)

Part 5

21 museum shop (As you can see, on your left here is the museum shop.)
22 pictures of the city (… on your right, you will see some pictures of the city.)
23 toilets (The toilets are also located on the first floor. They're right next to the lift.)
24 café (If you get hungry or thirsty, there's a café on the second floor.)
25 £5 (It costs £5.)

Test 3 Paper 3 Speaking

Part 2

Possible questions:

Art museum
What can you see (there)?
Is it open on Monday?
Is there a student ticket? How much does it cost?
Is there a car park?
What is the address?

Bike race
Where is it/the bike race?
When is it/the bike race?
Is it for children?
What is the website?
What can you win?

Test 4 Paper 1 Reading and Writing

Part 1

1 A   2 E   3 F   4 G   5 D

Part 2

6   B (*Called* means it is the name of the team.)
7   C (You *play for* a team.)
8   C (*But* introduces a contrast. The team is sometimes not very good. Therefore they sometimes lose.)
9   B (*Learnt a lot of things* means he/she has learnt a lot. *Ways* and *kinds* are both followed by *of*.)
10 C (We say it is *important to do* something.)

Part 3

11 B   12 C   13 C   14 A   15 B
16 A   17 G   18 B   19 F   20 C

Part 4

21 C
22 A (This piece of code can copy itself …)
23 A (Another unpleasant thing that can happen is that you get hundreds of spam emails every day.)
24 B (This can happen if you give your email address to people you don't know or to websites on the Internet.)
25 A (If they have your email address, they can send you a message that may contain false information.)
26 B (So, if you are using the Internet, you need to be careful that you do not put yourself in any danger.)
27 C

Part 5

28 C (*So much* is used to talk about quantity with uncountable nouns or when we don't have a noun, as is the case here. *So many* is used with countable nouns. *So far* is wrong.)
29 A (The correct preposition for *close* is *to*.)
30 B (*Was* is the correct form of the verb *to be* to use with the subject/in the past.)
31 A (A possessive adjective is needed here; one that refers to the writer.)
32 C (*For* is the time phrase to use for a period of time.)
33 A (The infinitive form is needed here.)
34 C (*Be used to* is followed by the verb form verb-*ing*.)
35 A (A link to show contrast is needed here.)

Part 6

36 watch   37 wallet   38 dress   39 raincoat   40 trainers

Part 7

41 him (An object pronoun referring to Peter is needed here.)
42 tell (A verb is needed here. *Tell* is correct because it takes an object.)
43 did (The past form of the verb *do* is needed here.)
44 be (The phrase is *to be able to do something*.)
45 the (The definite article is needed here.)
46 have (This clause is in the present perfect tense. The auxiliary verb *have* is needed here.)
47 you (A subject is needed here to complete the request.)
48 some (Milk is uncountable so needs the determiner *some*.)
49 will (The auxiliary verb *will* is needed here to refer to the future.)
50 see (A verb is needed here.)

Part 8

51 February 14th (The date of the concert is needed here.)
52 7.30 p.m. (The time of the concert is needed here.)
53 6.00/6 o'clock (Let's meet at your place at 6 o'clock.)
54 £30 (Students: £10 … Can you buy a ticket for my sister too?)
55 bus (We can then take the bus to the Open Arena.)

Part 9

Sample answer:
Hi Louise,
This year we're going to the beach for our holidays. Before we go, I'd love to come and stay with you.
I'm also going to stay with my cousin Katerina in the city.
Bye,
Maria

This answer is good because:
* it answers the three questions in the email from Louise.
* it clearly communicates the writer's message.
* it is between 25 and 35 words long (it is 33 words long).
* it is an informal email.

Test 4 Paper 2 Listening

Part 1

1 C (No, but we saw lions and giraffes.)
2 A (Bus stop 31 – it's the one after the pool.)
3 C (I think I've broken my leg … Oh, I think I've cut my hand too.)
4 C (And only yesterday it was sunny and mild.)
5 C (Yes, a coffee please. I've got some sandwiches with me for lunch but some biscuits with the coffee would be nice.)

Part 2

6 E (Now she just reads lots of magazines.)
7 C (My dad spends hours on his computer every night reading emails.)
8 A (She reads books.)
9 F (I think the only thing I've ever seen him read is a restaurant menu.)
10 G (Newspapers are definitely her thing.)

Part 3

11 B (On Friday night we went out for a meal.)
12 A (Then at 5 o'clock we went to see a film.)
13 C (We saw *Star Wars* – the first one.)
14 A (My cousins wouldn't stop talking all the way through it.)
15 B (Actually, no. They left this morning.)

Part 4

16 5th (No, this Friday is the 5th.)
17 Park (… we've arranged to have our practice at Smith Park.)
18 6.30 (I'd say we'll be finished by 6.30.)
19 parents (You'll need to tell your parents about it and they'll need to sign this form.)
20 6789022 (It's 6789022.)

21 3457700 (You can get tickets for both days from the box office or by phoning 3457700.)
22 £5 (Tickets cost £10 for adults and £5 for students and children.)
23 1567 (... send a text message to 1567 ...)
24 TFF (Write your name and TFF, for Teen Film Festival.)
25 Friday (We'll announce the lucky winners next Friday ...)

Test 4 Paper 3 Speaking

Part 2

Possible questions:

Animal hospital	Tennis lessons
What is the name of the animal hospital?	Where are they/the tennis lessons?
Is it open on Saturday?	Are they expensive?
Is it for horses?	Do I need a tennis racket?
Is there a car park?	Are there lessons on Sunday?
What is the address?	What is the phone number?

Test 5 Paper 1 Reading and Writing

Part 1

1 E   2 D   3 H   4 A   5 C

Part 2

6   C   (We say *most of the day* but *each day*; *more* is wrong here.)
7   A   (*Enjoys* goes with both *sunbathing* and *reading*.)
8   B   (You lie *under* an umbrella. The other prepositions of place are wrong.)
9   A   (The phrase *would like* is followed by the infinite with *to*. *Enjoy* is followed by verb-*ing* and *want* is wrong here.)
10 B   (We say I *can't wait* to do something.)

Part 3

11 A   12 B   13 A   14 A   15 A
16 A   17 D   18 B   19 G   20 F

Part 4

21 C   (I've got all sorts – from small ones I've found in magazines to very large ones I've bought at concerts or sporting events.)
22 A   (My favourite poster is one that I have of my favourite film – *The Lord of the Rings*. It's more than a metre high and I've put it up on my bedroom wall where I can see it when I'm lying in bed.)
23 B   (We started the group only last year, but we have already played five concerts – two of them at school!)
24 B   (Of course I'm not the only singer in the group. Melissa, one of the guitarists, also sings.)
25 C   (I really love my hobby and hope that when I grow up I will be in a famous band.)
26 B   (Every winter I go snowboarding with my father and my brother.)
27 B   (I'd like to try skateboarding because people tell me it's a little like snowboarding.)

Part 5

28 A   (*Because* introduces the reason she does not go to school.)
29 A   (*Has* is the correct choice for the third person present perfect.)
30 A   (*Youngest* is correct because the superlative of *young* is needed here.)
31 A   (*Other* is used with plural forms; *another* and *every* with singular forms.)
32 B   (*When* can be used like a relative pronoun that refers to time. Here it refers to when Nettie was 7 years old.)
33 A   (The simple past of the verb *to be* is needed here.)
34 A   (*Who* is a relative pronoun that refers to people. Here it refers to Nettie's teachers.)
35 C   (*But* introduces a contrast here.)

Part 6

36 fridge   37 clock   38 radio   39 television   40 lamp

Part 7

41 been (The past participle of the verb *to be* is needed here.)
42 play (*Play* collocates with *beach volleyball*.)
43 with (A preposition is needed here.)
44 having (You *have* a wonderful time.)
45 is (The verb *to be* is needed here.)
46 seen (You *see* a place.)
47 going (*Going to* refers to a future intention here.)
48 of (The phrase is *lots of*.)
49 you (An object pronoun is needed here.)
50 will (*Will* refers to the future here.)

Part 8

51 12th May (Monday 12th May)
52 (own) lunch (Bring your own lunch.)
53 7.30 (Let's meet at my place at 7.30 on Monday morning.)
54 bus (We can take the bus to school.)
55 car (She'll drive you home.)

Part 9

Sample answer:
<u>Lost</u>
I lost my new mobile phone in the cafeteria yesterday. It's a small black Samsung phone with a large screen. Please give it to Ms Smith in Room 10 if you find it.
Thanks,
Rachel.

This answer is good because:
• it deals with all three points.
• it clearly communicates the writer's message.
• it is between 25 and 35 words long (it is 33 words long).
• it is a note.

Test 5 Paper 2 Listening

Part 1

1 B (This one's on sale at the moment. From 750 Euros it's now down to 650.)
2 A (Now, I'm watching TV.)
3 A (Can you come to my office at 3.30?)
4 A (The 3rd? That's on Saturday.)
5 A (We're going to the Lake District. We'll be camping by the water.)

Part 2

6 C (On Thursday we had to vote between going horse-riding and going fishing and we all said we wanted to go horse-riding, so that's what we did.)
7 E (On Friday we went swimming in the lake.)
8 D (On Saturday we were going to play volleyball but it started to rain, so we hung around the camp and just played games all day.)
9 G (On Sunday we were going to play tennis but most of us wanted to play volleyball because we hadn't played the day before. So that's what we did.)
10 B (We were given a guided tour by the farmer.)

Part 3

11 B (This one will be my 9th.)
12 B (It's called *Fashion Week*.)
13 B (So, Tammy and I each paid £20 and we both got a game.)
14 C (We got it from a new place. It's called Small World.)
15 B (They also sell CDs and DVDs.)

Part 4

16 Sunday (Anyway, it's this Sunday.)
17 12.00/12 o'clock (At 12 o'clock.)
18 Banana Tree restaurant (We're having it at Banana Tree restaurant.)
19 Burgundy (B.U.R.G.U.N.D.Y.)
20 train (I'm not sure. You could take the train.)

Part 5

21 70 (There are 70 steps in all.)
22 (the) top (The entrance to the castle is at the top of the stairs.)
23 left (That will be our meeting point and where we will begin our tour – on the left as soon as you enter the castle.)
24 £5.50 (The tickets for the castle itself are £11 for adults and exactly half that price – £5.50 – for children.)
25 £7 (It costs £7)

Test 5 Paper 3 Speaking

Part 2

Possible questions:

<u>Photography classes</u>
Where are the classes?
When are the classes?
Do I/you need a camera?
What's the phone number?
How much do they cost?

<u>DVD club</u>
What is the name of the DVD club?
Where is the DVD club?
Can you rent games?
Is it open (on) Sundays?
Does it have a website?

Test 6 Paper 1 Reading and Writing

Part 1

1 A   2 H   3 E   4 G   5 B

Part 2

6 B (*Across* collocates with *the road*.)
7 C (The comparative form of *few* is needed here.)
8 A (A verb meaning *believe* or *think* is needed here.)
9 C (The phrase is *on foot*.)
10 A (*Takes* is used to refer to length of time.)

Part 3

11 A   12 C   13 A   14 B   15 C
16 C   17 G   18 D   19 A   20 E

Part 4

21 A (In the busy summer months Thanasis is a waiter in his family's restaurant.)
22 C (Because he is the only person in his family who can speak English, it his job to look after the tourists when they eat at the restaurant.)
23 A (... it is his job to look after the tourists when they eat at the restaurant.)
24 B (... he travels 12 kilometres every day by bus to a nearby village to go to school.)
25 A (Together with his classmates, two evenings a week, he attends English classes at a language school in the same village.)
26 C (He is very pleased that he can help his family in the summer ...)
27 A (What does Thanasis want to do when he grows up? He wants to own a restaurant, of course!)

28 C (*Than* is used in comparatives.)
29 A (*And* adds another similar idea.)
30 C (A subject pronoun is needed here.)
31 A (*Did* is added to negative simple past statements.)
32 B (The simple past of the verb *to be* is needed here.)
33 A (*Since* is used with a time in the past in present perfect sentences.)
34 B (The superlative form of *popular* is needed here.)
35 A (This is a prediction about the future. *Will* is used for predictions.)

Part 6

36 email   37 text   38 newspaper   39 diary   40 card

Part 7

41 why (*Why* introduces the reason she was not at school.)
42 to (*Come* is used with the preposition *to*.)
43 the (The definite article is needed here.)
44 please (The request is *Can you please let me know* …)
45 in (The preposition *in* is used with *the lesson*.)
46 will (*Will* is used to express a promise.)
47 sorry (*I'm sorry* can be used to express sympathy.)
48 hope (*I hope* is used to express a wish.)
49 do (A verb is needed here; one that collocates with *work*.)
50 you (An object pronoun is needed here.)

Part 8

51 Giles (To: Jill Giles <j.giles@uk.com>)
52 15 (Happy 15th!)
53 29/09 (Sent: Thurs 29/09 … Today I sent that amazing photo …)
54 j.giles@uk.com (To: Jill Giles <j.giles@uk.com>)
55 a sunset (Today I sent that amazing photo of the sunset you took to a photo competition.)

Part 9

Sample answer:
Hi Matt,
As you can see, my town is also big. I love going to the beach, which is near my house. At weekends, I enjoy going swimming with my family and friends.
Bye,
Tom.

This answer is good because:
- it answers all three questions in Matthew's email.
- it clearly communicates the writer's message.
- it is between 25 and 35 words long (it is 31 words long).
- it is an informal email.

Test 6 Paper 2 Listening

Part 1

1 A (We were expecting around 25 but only 18 ended up coming.)
2 B (I made some spaghetti.)
3 C (It's square so it will fit nicely in the corner and it's big.)
4 C (Well, there's my mum and dad, my grandfather, my sister, Tania, and my brother Mario. … There are six of us in all.)
5 A (So straight down here. Turn left at the corner and it's on my left as soon as I've turned?)

Part 2

6   D (I got a CD from my sister.)
7   B (My grandma got me a book.)
8   G (Tony bought me a T-shirt.)
9   H (Penny said she was going to get me the same T-shirt but she changed her mind at the last minute and bought me a video game.)
10 E (He got me a pair of jeans like the ones we saw him wearing at his party.)

Part 3

11 B   (It's about a girl called Matilda ...)
12 A   (We saw it at the cinema on George Street.)
13 C   (Well, it actually doesn't start till quarter to seven.)
14 C   (I'll go on Sunday.)
15 A   (Actually I think I read it's only £5 on Sundays.)

Part 4

16 Tuesday (They're on every Tuesday and Thursday at 6.00.)
17 7.30 (No, they last for an hour and a half. We finish at 7.30.)
18 £45 (It's £45 a month.)
19 5678900 (Yes, it's 5678900.)
20 Delon (D.E.L.O.N.)

Part 5

21 2.30 (... at half past two every Saturday afternoon.)
22 Saturday (... at half past two every Saturday afternoon.)
23 five/5 (Every week the show's presenters will answer five of your questions.)
24 £50 (If you're right, you could win £50.)
25 people (Three people will have a chance to win £50 each week.)

Test 6 Paper 3 Speaking

Part 2

Possible questions:
New computer game
What is the name of the game?
Where can you buy it?
How many players can play?
Is it for children?
How much does it cost?

New film
What is the name of the film?
Where can you see it?
Is it for teenagers?
Can you go on Sunday?
What time is it on?